THE ROSE AND THE STONE

To Bill
with love
& kindest
affection

Peter

First published 2013

ISBN: 978-1482558364

The thoughts and ideas contained in this book are universal and thus do not belong to anyone in particular. Please feel free to use the content in any way you see fit, but an acknowledgement is always welcome.

For more information about the author, please visit *www.patthebarber.com*

Cover photograph by John Minihan

Prepared for publication by
MAURICE SWEENEY PUBLISHING SERVICES
Ballyhillow, Leap, Co. Cork, Ireland

THE ROSE AND THE STONE

*'The rose makes public what was
always private in the stone.'*
JOHN MORIARTY

PAT *THE BARBER* CROWLEY

Contents

INTRODUCTION	1

ONCE BORN

CHILDHOOD DAYS	11
MYSTERIES OF LIFE	17
A SILENT FEAR	21

TWICE BORN

THE ROSE AND THE STONE	27
TRUE SELF	29
BOUNDARIES AND SEPARATIONS	33
BLUE PLANET LIVING	40
HILLSIDE HAPPENINGS	43
GENTLY UPON THE EARTH	53
UNHEALTHY EGO	58
LIVING AND DYING	63
NOT INVOLVED	73
WORSHIPPING FALSE GODS	78
YOU ARE SAFER THAN YOU THINK	81
ORDINARY OR EXTRAORDINARY?	83
THE WAY WE ARE	85
CHILDLIKE LOVE	95
SPIRITUAL PIONEERS	97
REACTING AND RESPONDING	102
HEART BUSINESS ONLY	106
OUR SLEEP OF EARTH	110

WHO ARE YOU?	116
ETERNITY IS NOW	121
A THIRST UNQUENCHED	128
GREAT AND SMALL	132
OUR FORMER GLORY	139
LOVE CHILD	144
ME THINKING	147
WHEN LISTENING HAPPENS	149
PARK BENCH THINKING	155
INSIDE OUT IMAGININGS	160
THE BUTTERFLY	162
WHEN SHADOWS FALL	164
THE POVERTY OF MORE	170
WORDS, SPIRITUALITY, AND TRUTH	173

INTRODUCTION

by Perry O'Donovan

In questioning or inquiring, says Pat Crowley in one of the early sections of this remarkable collection of writings, "I am turning my face for home and towards the source of my true nature."

This book has been 20 years in the making—rather, it should be said that it has been a *lifetime* in the making, but that parts of it were first set down in the 1990s at the encouragement of Pat's friend and guiding spirit the poet and seer John Moriarty. Indeed, the title 'The Rose and the Stone'— '. . . the rose makes public what was always private in the stone . . .'—is a Moriarty composition.

Starting out Pat describes growing up in Castlehaven—which is in west Cork, south of Skibbereen—in 1950s rural Ireland, emerging from the cocoon of a hillside, smallholding household to encounter the ignorant cruelties of the schoolhouse, the mysteries and frailties of the church, and—later—the consolations of sport and music and the holiday fug and babble of the crowded public houses in the nearby seaside villages; a journey along the bog-tracks and goat-paths that take us from a world without boundaries or divisions—a world wherein even animals and humans are of equal importance—to a time and place where we are

1

conscripted to live in the "poverty of human ideas, concepts, and beliefs".

The following, from the 'Mysteries of life' section, gives a good sense of Pat's very down-to-earth way of approaching his subject-matter (pp. 21-2):

"Living by the church, I saw all the funerals and as an altar boy I served at funeral masses and saw at first hand the great heartbreak and grief brought about by death. My father, being a man of the shovel and pick—and living near the cemetery—was often asked to dig the graves. I would help out with this work, which often included gathering up the remains of human bones in old shallow graves so as to dig to the required depth for the new coffin. Later, at the funeral service, I would hear the priest speak of the person being raised up on the last day. Now I knew that those bones I had seen in the graveyard were going nowhere . . . That the human body dies was obvious enough, that the human does not survive death in any shape or form was also obvious. The body, once buried in the ground, disintegrated and was slowly but surely absorbed into the soil without any chance of survival whatsoever . . . The teaching and the reality I experienced did not add up."

Pat left school early (just 14 years old) and apprenticed in a barber shop—hence "the Barber", the name by which he is colloquially known in his hometown and its surrounds.

At weekends he played in a music group, The Peptones, one of the earliest pop-groups in the locality (he played with other groups afterwards but The Peptones was the original of these entertainment line-ups). These were the years of the first great wave of modern-day tourism in Ireland—the age of the picture-postcard, Joe O'Reilly horse-drawn caravans and Homecoming Festivals, and west Cork so unspoilt that, for example, in *The Coast of West Cork* (1972), in cycling the dozen or so miles between Skibbereen and Ballydehob, Peter Somerville-Large records encountering just *two* motorized vehicles.

Pat was a teenager in the 1960s and, in the '70s, with shoulder-length hair and *Rolling Stone* style, a married man with a pretty wife and two young children of his own.

But the 1980s brought about a revolution in Pat's life—a great crisis of selfhood—a crisis that first undid him and afterwards, grasping a new soil, made him anew.

"Some persons are born with an inner constitution which is harmonious and well balanced from the outset", says William James in his foundational *Varieties of Religious Experience: A Study in Human Nature* (1902), "[their] impulses are consistent with one another, their will follows without trouble the guidance of their intellect, their passions are not excessive, and their lives are little haunted by regrets. Others are oppositely constituted; and are so in degrees which may vary from something so slight as to result in a merely odd or whimsical inconsistency, to a discordancy of which the consequences may be inconvenient in the extreme. . . . [persons] whose existence is little more than a series of zigzags, as now one tendency and now another gets the upper hand. Their spirit wars with their flesh, they wish for incompatibles, wayward impulses interrupt their most deliberate plans, and their lives are one long drama of repentance and of effort to repair misdemeanors and mistakes." These are folks who to know any peace or happiness at all must—as James puts it—be "twice-born": people for whom there are two lives, the natural and the spiritual, and they must die to the one before they can participate in the other.

The gentle guidance and fellowship of two local old boys, Beara's Jim Harrington and Kealkill's Con Keohane—returned immigrants who'd spent most of their working lives in London—put Pat in the way of the first glimmer of spiritual enlightenment (see, for example, the sketch in the 'Hillside happenings' section, pp. 43-52). But both these homespun savants died within months of one another, leaving Pat alone again, a fledging in this newfound dimension, lost and stumbling in the soupy fog, headed nowhere, apparently, for no good reason.

Then one day—with darkness visible—Pat's wife Marion handed him a copy of the *RTE Guide*—the listings magazine for Ireland's national broadcasting service—"I think you'll be interested in this", she said as she handed it to him. And she was right: the cover-story was a trailer for a new TV series, 'The Blackbird and the Bell', which centred on the writer and mystic and sometime-gardener/sometime-academic John Moriarty.

Kerryman John Moriarty (1938-2007) was a graduate of University College, Dublin—a double-first in philosophy and literature—who, after postgraduate studies at Leeds, lectured on the western literary canon at the University of Manitoba in Winnipeg in Canada for a number of years. In the 1970s, however, Moriarty turned his back on the academic life and, *à la* [the Spanish saint] John of the Cross, became a live-in gardener in a Carmelite monastery. After a few years of this (where his ebullient table-talk and full-bodied story-telling had become renowned), Moriarty returned to Ireland and built a little dwelling for himself on a plot of land he'd been gifted in Roundstone, county Galway, on the west coast of Ireland.

And it was here—having driven up from west Cork to seek him out—that Pat first met the great Kerry mystic—"A large, rough-hewn man with bright, deep set eyes beneath a leonine mass of curls"—sheltering from an April downpour under a wind-blown whitethorn. These were great flowering years for Moriarty too—all the publications for which he is celebrated date from his Connemara days onward: *Dreamtime* (1994) the *Turtle* trilogy (1996, 1997, 1998), *Anaconda Canoe* (1999), *Nostos*, (2001), *Invoking Ireland* (2005), *Night Journey to Buddh Gaia* (2006) and *What the Curlew Said* (2007). The two men became fast friends and, a little while later, when Moriarty removed to his native Kerry to realise his long-cherished dream of establishing 'Sli na Firinne', a Christian monastic 'hedge school' in the Mangerton Mountains near Killarney, it was Pat in his VW van who ferried him and all his belongings south to the holy ground.

"John both rooted and expanded my awareness in ways that no words can describe," says Pat, "the man was a fountainhead of insight and inspiration." Nevertheless, while words are wind "without men like London Con [Keohane], Spiritual Jim [Harrington], and John Moriarty I do not think I would have found the way at all—people have to carry the message", which is why this book.

In a lovely passage that could very well stand for the collection as a whole (p. 82) Pat writes— "There are people who seem quite content with their lot in life, and [there are] those who are not, who feel afraid, vulnerable, and discontent, seeking answers, wondering if this is all there is [to life]. Whether in the shape of a belief system or some philosophy, we give them still more words, and still they feel lost and alone . . . It is to these people that this [book] may be of interest, those who seek even though they know not what . . . The writing itself is just so many words; what it contains is beyond all words, symbols and thought, and beyond all that you will ever know, because you cannot know what you truly are, you can only *be* it. In truth, there is nothing to be done and no-one to do it. Just *be*, you are safer than you think—all is well and all is very well."

Church Meadow House, Skibbereen
February 2013

ONCE BORN

CHILDHOOD DAYS

Being born into a family of six children in a small cottage set in a rural valley less than one and a half miles from the sea, I grew up in a world closely intertwined with nature. In fact, as a child, this was my only world, and nothing as far as I could see was remotely more important than the land and all it gave us: our food and water and the wood for the Stanley No 8 range on which our mother did all our cooking. Mother Nature was the great provider. The animals and the humans were of equal importance, and for me the outside world had as yet imposed no boundaries or divisions, nor was I as yet conscripted to live in the poverty of human ideas, concepts, and beliefs. The world of words and outside structures that awaited the young boy had at this time no meaning in my childhood valley and surrounding hills. I was at one with nature and in love with all. The cruelties of life and its often strangely cruel humans were hidden from my childhood world where the love for our collie dog was so fulfilling and comforting that paradise was always mine and mine alone.

This was a childhood of doing and helping, feeding the hens, fetching water from the well, and milking the goats which we kept on a neighbour's hill. The hill stood straight south from our front door and on its highest point stood a large stone fort which had a small opening on its south-eastern side. This was ideal for milking the goats which were first rounded up with the help of the collie dog and, once inside the high-walled ring fort, the milking could be done with relative ease. Outside the small opening some large flat stone flags lay on the ground. One stone flag in particular had shallow round holes chiselled on its surface, and into these we would pour some milk for the dog. I have since learned that they were in fact burial stones similar to those found in Middle Eastern countries. On the north side of the entrance a small chamber was built into the fort wall and here we often sheltered from the south westerly wind and the rain that blew in from the Atlantic ocean to the south. This was truly a young boy's paradise. It gave a feeling of great safety as the surrounding countryside fell away on all sides.

My childhood curiosity ran wild and I was always full of questions, often to the annoyance of my father and mother. Sometimes my questions were easily answered, except that there were so many. I needed to know how everything worked, like how did all the wild flowers get here and where did they come from, who put them there and where did all the colours came from. Everywhere I looked I had a question. I think when I turned my attention to the sky and all it held, my parents were in big trouble, and the only fact I established was that the man in the moon was watching me. Around this time also, I was informed that a creature called the Boogey Man was waiting and watching to get me if I ventured anywhere I was told not to, especially after dark. Next came God—he was also watching over me to keep me safe, but if I did anything wrong he would see my sins and be very angry, and the danger was I could end up in hell. Well informed I was not, but well watched I certainly was!

Next came school and the painful experience of being confined and being hit by a stranger for the first time; the pain is as present to me now as if it were recorded in stone. For the first time I was made aware of my great emotional sensitivity. It was indeed a strange education, where the first lesson I learned well was to dislike with all my heart. My soul screamed out in anguish at being a prisoner of the stranger, suffering the humiliation of having to cry openly in front of other children and being held up for all to see as a good example of stupidity. For the rest of my book-learning days, I knew in my heart of hearts that I wasn't stupid, yet I could not learn. My one and only ambition at school was to get out as quickly as possible, and I did. I have always felt that

13

violence of the tongue causes just as much psychological damage as physical violence. In secondary school it seemed to be part of the scheme of things to humiliate the student in order to make him teachable. At this time I sported a Beatle hairstyle which was not very long except that the fringe was cut short above the line of the eyebrows. The headmaster called me an insect and never by my first name. Another teacher liked to tell me that it was a fine thing my father reared a greyhound instead of me. I longed to be free and after much persuading of my parents I was apprenticed before my fifteenth birthday to a barber and was free at last. My big enjoyment in life was football and all kind of sport. However, Gaelic football and music were my great passions.

Living as we did in our cottage within a stone's throw from the school and church, I was almost a professional altar boy, serving not just the Sunday masses but weddings and funerals also, as well as the morning masses celebrated by different priests on holidays. This I really enjoyed. It gave me a feeling of well-being that I needed so much. I got on well with all the priests, who were very kind to me. Sometimes the priests on holiday would give me a present before returning to their own parishes in different countries. There was one local priest I was particularly fond of. He drove an Austin A40 which rarely exited second gear. Only one or two people in our valley had a car at this time but all were in agreement that the priest was the worst driver on the road. He was often late for 8 o'clock mass on Sunday mornings. The women would be sitting inside the church but most of the men and myself would be waiting outside listening for the first sounds of the Austin. If the wind was blowing in from the sea to the south, he would be heard approaching while still a quarter of a mile away, the accelerator pressed hard to the floor and second gear all the way. Once he came into view coming down the Coondubh Hill, all would scatter and pretend everything was normal. In the sacristy everything would be ready with the help of an old lady, Lill Daly, who also rang the bell. She lived in the next valley north of ours. We would have his vestments laid out on the press where they were kept, and part of my brief was to make sure that when he put them on they were straight and pulled down at the back. Then would come the fastest mass in the South West. This was probably one reason why the church was always full at eight on Sunday morning.

As altar boys we had to stay very alert while answering in Latin because he often left out some of the less important parts and rarely gave a sermon, and if he did it was short and sweet. Everybody loved him, and not just for his short mass. He was a gentle, kind man and it was only many years later

15

I learned that he was an alcoholic. My parents never said these things openly. They would speak of him in whispered tones and would usually add "Ah, God love him." Often when he failed to arrive for early mass, someone who had a car would be dispatched to his house to get him. There is something uncommonly special about people who unthinkingly combine to support the less able in the community. To accept, as these people did, the fragility and vulnerability of this man's earthly humanness, regardless of their own needs and expectations, displays a spirituality and humility that illuminates the darkest recesses of humankind.

When he died, his body was buried in the church grounds near the front door where we had often waited for him on Sunday mornings. He remains to this day the only person to be buried there. How little I realised at this time that I too would be sentenced to walk the hard lonely road of alcoholism. Passing through the teenage years, a feeling of something being very wrong within me began to surface, the feelings of inadequacy and of not really being a part of all that was happening in everyday life. The games of youth could no longer mask the empty feeling inside. I felt isolated and alone within myself. Unconsciously, I had learned to cover up these feelings by being funny and devil-may-care. I took up drinking in my late teens and discovered the answer to all that ailed me. When I took a drink the lights came on inside. I no longer felt uncomfortable or ill at ease. This was the feeling I had always wanted—how I could have done with a drink that first day at school. I was up and running at last and so began a roller coaster ride that lasted for twenty years.

MYSTERIES OF LIFE

Standing one day on the hillsides of my youth, the eyes that looked upon the timeless scenes of childhood were the eyes of a free man. For the first time in adulthood there was hunger in my looking and wondering in my heart. My childhood curiosity of the world about me had returned. Free now from the crippling chains of active alcoholism, there was a clarity and a sensitivity that felt very strange and wonderful. Everything looked very different, felt different, and sounded different. Once again, these quiet places held a magic I had not experienced since childhood. Whenever an opportunity arose, I would be drawn to some of the timeless places I had known as a boy. I would often feel that I was looking for something, yet I didn't have any words or names to put on the feelings within, and most of my attention at this stage centred on the world outside. Once again, I was full of questions and a longing to know more about life. I felt I needed to know these things and that somehow I must know.

Even as a young boy I felt frustrated and annoyed if I could not understand something or if I failed to receive a satisfactory answer to my many questions. Now, as then, to believe in something I can't understand seems like nonsense. I often felt amazed that others seemed to accept concepts they were told to believe in without question. I had plenty of questions and when the answers I received failed to add up, I rejected the beliefs. Now having walked the crooked, narrow road of a partial life, I had at last arrived at a place where my questions held no guilt, only wonderment and sincerity. To find the truth and nothing but the truth seemed to me the most important reason for life. Of course, the everyday business of living was also important but somehow that was on the surface of life. My quest for truth, for the answers to the mysteries of life, from the smallest to the greatest, held my every waking thought. I searched for clues in everything I touched, in every life experience that presented itself to my consciousness. In the East they say that a teacher or guru is necessary for enlightenment while others claim that the most important guru is the one within. This guide within was always, it seemed, one step ahead. Whether I needed people or books, they would appear with the least effort on my part. This may give the impression that seeking enlightenment is an easy ride. Nothing could be further from the truth. There were times I wished I could accept life like most people I knew, who were reasonably happy to accept the obvious and leave it at that. Many times I tried to divert my attention to the issues on the surface just to escape the intense frustration and the unavoidable confrontation with the truth, with reality. However, I would soon find myself once again totally immersed in attempting to solve the most outrageous and often tragic contradictions of life.

It was about this time that, quite unexpectedly, first one person and then another came strolling into my life. Both were the living answers to all my longings. Now my questioning mind was propelled on to a higher level of expectation. Now at last I had found someone who had answers and during our many conversations the deep longings which had been with me since childhood were beginning to be fulfilled. Jim had been turbo-charged into enlightenment courtesy of a profound spiritual experience. Con, on the other hand, became enlightened by direct self-inquiry. Jim was quiet and gentle and spoke little while Con held nothing back. Blessed with a brilliant mind, he was forceful and spoke with authority. In their company I was elevated, sometimes unknowingly, onto another level of inquiry and expectation. Then sadly they were gone with the same suddenness with which they had arrived. Both had shed their bodies within five weeks of one another, and less than two years of our first meeting. No words I could summon would adequately describe the loss and loneliness I felt at their passing. There was so much more I needed to know, so many questions I hadn't yet asked. I desperately needed further explanations of the things they had said. But they were gone and the darkness fell around me with no promise of a new dawn. There is a darkness that the light of common day cannot brighten. Our often fragile human spirit can be quenched in an instant, leaving behind a life that seems useless. There is also a loneliness that all human endeavours and the kindest words fail to alleviate. The restless human soul lies abandoned and alone, unlit by anything our earthly senses can offer.

It was during a particularly low period following the deaths of my two friends that John Moriarty appeared from the wilds of rural Ireland, except he didn't leave the wild behind him, because physically, psychologically, and spiritually, and whether he liked it or not, wildness was something he couldn't walk away from.

Almost instantly I felt sheltered. His big-heartedness comforted me, his Intelligence inspired me, and his earthiness returned me once again to the open door of Mother Earth. Strangely, however, much of our conversation centred on our love of Gaelic football and the ancient tribal enmity between our respective counties of Cork and Kerry. Instead of being something negative and destructive, it ignited a passion which brought otherwise mostly passive peoples to their feet, to the edge of their seats, and to the very edge of life itself, where nothing else mattered except the living moment of battle. In a odd way the boundary lines that divided us also united us in the spirit of the warrior. John and I had differences and similarities in equal measure regarding our respective approaches to spirituality, life, and mysticism. What united us was a heartfelt love for the miracle of existence and all that existence came wrapped up in.

A SILENT FEAR

The fear of death was very real to me since childhood. The reality of this devastating and final end was very much a part of life in our valley. Living by the church, I saw all the funerals and as an altar boy I served at funeral masses and saw at first hand the great heartbreak and grief brought about by death. My father, being a man of the shovel and pick and living near the cemetery, was often asked to dig graves. I would help out with this work, which often included gathering up the remains of human bones in old shallow graves so as to dig to the required depth for the new coffin. Later, at the funeral service, I would often hear the priest speak of the person being raised up on the last day. Now I knew that the bones I had often seen in the graveyard were not going anywhere. The teaching and the reality I had experienced did not add up. When my brother of eighteen years died from cancer, the full horror of death became a shattering experience. The inconsolable grief of my parents and older sisters stunned me into silence for over two weeks. This is a condition that is often part of human experience and which I can only describe as a "black sea of pain". Those who have been there will know well what I mean. When we begin to emerge from this grievously wounding state we are like a leaf in the autumn breeze and at the mercy of greater forces. To have experienced this pain is to have known a powerlessness that can't be held in any words or known through any teaching. It can only be known at an experiential level and for the experiencer life may never be the same again. Death is what we spend most of our time pushing away. Consciously or unconsciously, this forms the background for a great deal of our activities. It is also one of the reasons why we have great difficulty living in the now. We mostly live in our chosen projected future, but our certain future is death, our only guarantee from the outset. To spend our lives whistling past the graveyard, pretending we are not afraid, is to live a life where we are always on the run and seldom if ever take our rest.

To have an interest in the many great questions of life also means having an interest in death. I could never be satisfied with any of the answers I received concerning death. Most people, as far as I could see, were not really interested in discussing the subject. Once I was free to inquire into life and God with an open mind, birth and death formed a vitally important part of the inquiry. That the body did not survive death in any shape or form was obvious. The body, once buried in the ground, disintegrated and was slowly but surely absorbed into the soil without any chance of survival whatsoever. The same could be said for cremation. So what, if anything, survived the death of the body? If there was a life after the death of my body, what was it, where was it, and how could it be? These were the questions that were constantly presenting themselves as I continued to inquire into the age-old mysteries of life.

TWICE BORN

THE ROSE AND THE STONE

The rose makes public what was always private in the stone
—John Moriarty

Who would have thought that the stone hides a secret that a rose cannot keep to itself? What, you may ask, is the relationship? Surely there is no comparison between the deadness of the stone and the unbridled liveliness of the rose? The rose says "Look at me, see what energy I have", while the stone stays silent.

Love also has its silence and privacy. That's the thing about love: it speaks its truth silently yet powerfully, regardless of what I think or understand. Perhaps this unspoken privacy, this wordless love is what the rose speaks of.

The story of the rose and the stone may be also our story. Is it not the case that we are unable to hide what we love the most about ourselves. We love and enjoy our aliveness more than anything else; our feeling of being present, being conscious, is our most treasured possession which we would not trade for anything or anyone. This is what we love the most, and yet in the same way as the stone holds a secret most privately, there is something about ourselves also that feels hidden from our innermost feeling of aliveness. The rose and the stone by their very outward natures seem to be set apart like the pillars of an ancient temple erected in praise of some far-off god. Suppose, however, that our ancient gods are not as far off as we have been led to believe. Hidden from our eyes and our own outwardly manifest world they may well appear to be, but the world outside our eyes is not the only world we are related to. There is another world closer to us than our breathing, and whichever direction we take through life it walks right along with us and remains in constant attendance.

If the aliveness that beautifies the rose is also privately present in the stone, then perhaps the problem is not so much in the fact that it is hidden but has more to do with the direction we find ourselves looking in. For the way we look at the world, which is not the only way of looking, burdens us with the cross of short-sightedness, yet it is one we are always reluctant to lay down. This heavy cross is lightened, however, by the smiling rose that speaks unashamedly of something that has passed into privacy in our heart. Our blindness has turned our loving hearts to stone, and the living godlike beauty we are eternally acquainted with lies hidden from our eyes. But true seeing demands of us only that we turn inward and acknowledge all that is not made public enough for earthly eyes. Our hearts are trying to tell us that eyesight is not the only sight we are gifted with. Our intuitive intelligence stands ready and willing to lay bare the true brightness and beauty of our eternal aliveness, that the world outside our eyes in its blindness is ever unable to fully unfold.

TRUE SELF

Very many people are searching for spirituality, or something we call spirituality. Perhaps this searching has always taken place, except that in the wonderful times we now find ourselves in there are many more avenues of exploration to help us accommodate this longing. The very fact that religions and religious structures sprung up and became established in the past is itself testament to some collective longing and neediness. This searching is not confined to any nation or particular culture. It transcends all boundaries, all differences, great or small. It would also appear that it has always existed, even in the earliest cultures.

So what is this calling that asks the human heart to reach out to something that lies beyond all that our human heads

29

are capable of supplying? Thinking and intellectuality surely have never had it so good. Seldom has there been a time when they have been so prized, being elevated almost to the level of the gods and maybe for some cultures the intellect has replaced the notion of God entirely.

Still the calling continues from somewhere beyond all that intellect can offer. It appears to be at once coming from somewhere outside and yet so intimately from somewhere inside. Perhaps this is a very important point; maybe what we generally take as being outside is in fact more inside. Now if there is an intimacy that is not limited by individuality, and all that the feeling of being an individual implies, would it not also be fair to describe this intimacy as being collective? Still, in our narrow world of sensory perceptions, to be part of something that transcends individuality and separateness is beyond imagining and all reason.

Being greatly addicted, as we mostly are, to the feeling of individuality, of being separate from one another, we are mostly unwilling to embrace anything that threatens our individual existence. Understandable as this may be, even a primary investigation will suggest that these feelings and convictions are not the whole story.

When Descartes announced "I think, therefore I am" he was just plain wrong. Had he investigated the matter a little deeper, he may have realised his error and then his statement would have read "I am, therefore there is thinking." Firstly all intelligence is not limited to nor dependent on intellectuality or reason. Nor is all intelligence secondary to rational thought and thinking. One does not have to think to realise or confirm that one exists.

Thought is a movement in consciousness, and therefore consciousness precedes thought and also fills the gaps between thoughts. Furthermore, consciousness is the constant background which allows the three states of waking, dreaming, and dreamless sleep to alternate with one another. Now this solid background of consciousness-awareness is not one piece for me, a separate piece for you, and so on. This is the very heart of the matter. Consciousness-awareness is not private property, it is collective and universal, and is beyond and before all our imaginary divisions and separations which appear spontaneously in the relative world of Duality.

> *Individuality dissolves into boundless being, where death is an almost laughable impossibility*
>
> ALFRED LORD TENNYSON

What then is it that lies at the heart of our longing and vulnerability, that walks with us on our outward journey upon our blue Planet Earth? Something is obviously wrong. Something ails us, and despite our best efforts to shake it off, it continues to call us like some distant lover who sails freely into our innermost being and captivates our attention. Perhaps what ails us is our neglect of awareness, our halfheartedness to being, and our addiction to becoming. Living as we mostly do, high up in our heads, we view some distant hills as being so much greener than home; in the world of our busy heads all looking is outwards looking— the eye can see everything but cannot see itself. Awareness likewise, when reduced to self-consciousness, is always outward bound and so loses the run of itself and, just like the eye, it can only view all that itself it is not, but never what it itself is. Its calling is a longing for glories it has once known, yet whenever it searches it fails to find itself. What then is to be done? The answer is: nothing. All doing is still outward doing from somewhere in our lofty heads. Only when Being is allowed to climb down into itself, and becoming no longer holds sway, does the human heart become still. This stillness, the source of our very being, can never know itself, it can never find itself, because it can only be itself, and this itself is our true self always.

BOUNDARIES AND SEPARATIONS

As with all conversations about mysticism, whether spoken or written, it is essential to bear in mind that these words are in themselves merely pointers to the divine ground, our home. We may very well understand intellectually every word that has ever been put to paper regarding this subject but we are still in possession of second-hand information only. If the truth is to be grasped at all then only our intuitive intelligence can come to our rescue and, in one unannounced moment, grant us an understanding beyond all words and teaching. There is also, of course, the possibility of a transcendental or spiritual experience which often changes the recipient profoundly so that their life or view of life may never be the same again.

If we are asked to accept a set of answers or a philosophy, and the emphasis is centred around believing what is being said, then we are being asked to accept what is, at best, second-hand information. This is precisely what most people have immense difficulty with—believing something they are unable to verify for themselves. Indeed, with most organised teaching, to question is to be labelled a non-believer. Yet to be curious is part of humanity; perhaps curiosity is life in expression and life is spirit, love, and awareness uncensored. It is important that we ask questions without restriction not alone of others, teachers included, but also of ourselves, for the questions we ask of ourselves may well be the most important and liberating of all. First-hand information comes from oneself and oneself alone, direct experience is my experience and mine alone. This is our greatest blessing and helps awareness to shine forth as love in all its splendour. When I am asked to question, I am turning my face for home and towards the source of my true nature.

Once we are guided to open our hearts and minds to life, we also open the door to death and the whole concept of living and dying. Surely here is a more open and hugely different way of living. Imagine for a moment that the type of inquiry we are suggesting here were to be an integral part of education from the earliest age—in fact the earlier in our lives this sort of questioning is encouraged the better, because it is there in our childhood curiosity already. Then, instead of all the workings of life taking us away from our centre, we could live from our centre, our source, our consciousness. When daily life takes us journeying away from our father's house, we are being amused and bemused by the workings of the world about us, but all the while our homeland slips unknowingly into the mist of distant time. All goes well until perhaps one day we find ourselves washed up on the shores of life, stranded and immobilised by some uninvited crisis. What if, however, we were guided and encouraged to remain close to home by being initiated into ourselves and out of ourselves? Then we could travel outward as if we were tethered by a great invisible elastic rope that always brought us back safely to our own door. How different then would be our thoughts of life and death, for now we would cease erecting great barriers between living and dying. Then there would emerge a more realistic understanding of what I truly am, being no longer under the illusion of only being a human being, a person suffering from what Carl Jung once described as "the regrettable small of the soul".

Perhaps one of the greatest tragedies of past unenlightened thinking that has blighted the Western mind has been the notion that some distant god has the capacity to influence in some way our shady little souls. This belief continues to alienate mankind from its true source and at the same time erects boundaries between human and what man has called God, boundaries that in truth do not exist. This uninformed way of thinking is the underlying core out of which springs our dread of death. On one side of our self-made boundary stands all that we think to be real—that is, whatever is obvious to our senses of sight, hearing, touch, taste, and mind.

On the other imaginary side lies the unknown ground of all our human fears and misunderstandings concerning death and what we call the afterlife. Perhaps it is important here to awaken to ourselves to one misunderstanding regarding what we consider to be the unknown. I cannot in truth be afraid of something I don't know, because the ego or thinking centre can only fear the loss of the known. Returning to our self-erected boundaries, Ken Wilber states that "every boundary line becomes a potential battle line", so the conflicts within ourselves are nearly always of our own making. How, then, are we to escape from this unhappy state of affairs?

Here again only the understanding of our misendeavours can liberate us by simply revealing the falseness of our imaginary boundaries. There is little benefit in working to break down what is imaginary. When I see the false for what it is, then only the true remains. We are not just the persons we think we are, because this feeling of being a person is strictly relative. When the physical body combines with the five senses and the mind, our earthly prison is then ready to receive its captive who is guilty of no crime. The collective social viewpoint further abuses the innocence and slams shut the prison door. What happens is that awareness unbounded, which is what we are, is reduced to self-consciousness. The key has been thrown away and here we will remain, trying to make the best of our lot and always hoping that on some distant tomorrow things will be better and happiness will be ours. We expend much time and energy in learning and reflecting on the art of living, which is certainly praiseworthy, but we sorely neglect the art of dying, and while the art of living and the art of dying would at first appear to be at opposite ends of the spectrum, they are in fact the two sides of the one coin. Perhaps it is fair to say that taking living to an art form is not possible without opening our hearts and heads to the art of dying also.

The physical death of the body is not, of course, the only death that life demands we learn to deal with. To live a peaceful, harmonious life, we must also die to all our yesterdays, otherwise we will be unable to live freely in the now—and maybe learning to live is also learning to die, and vice versa. When we sleep we gladly die to everything we know and possess. We accept it without the slightest concern, yet the death of the body appals us and fills us with anxiety and an intense desire to prevent it from happening at all costs. Imagine, however, if we had the courage to see life and death as they truly are, an experience, sometimes happy, sometimes sorrowful, but still only an experience in consciousness. The individual I take myself to be is imaginary; there cannot in truth be a separate entity with free will called a person. The body that I take to be me is a chance happening from beginning to end, dependent on all the elements of what we call nature. It is also a product of these elements, and when it finally breaks down and dies it will dissolve back into that from which it came. Death is merely a change in the world of appearances, and life is also an ever-changing scene in our world of movie-like relative appearances. What is unchanging, without beginning or end, however, is the background without which all of these appearances could not take place—the pure spirit, godlike awareness which remains unaffected by all of the many changing events in our earthly world. Whatever takes place in our so-called real world is totally dependent on this unchanging background of awareness, in the same way that the reflection of the sun in a dew drop would not be possible without the sun.

Imagine, then, if we were able to stand on this earthly floor with an intuitive understanding of our true nature, how different would be our whole approach to the art of living and dying. Surely only true understanding can afford us true compassion for ourselves and others and the bodies we have become so wrapped up in. Now, the magical psychic worlds that visit us from time to time could take their proper place in this mystery of existence, and standing free as awareness, love, spirit, and eternal life, we would open our hearts and our more than personal consciousness to all that comes our way. My friend is dying of cancer, or is he? With our new-found understanding, let us attempt to clarify this situation. That the body he takes himself to be is breaking down remains beyond doubt. When the body stops operating and can no longer support the life force, then we call that body dead. Our problem begins when we consider the life force, the conscious awareness, to also have died. We wrongly assume that our feeling of being, of awareness, is dependent on the body for its continuing existence. It is not. That feeling of beingness is not dependent on anything for its existence, but is prior to all births and bodies; indeed, all physical bodies are totally dependent and reliant upon spirit awareness for their functioning and existence.

What happens to the person, the personality that I feel I am and have become wrapped up in all these years? Will this also die? The answer is that it doesn't. How could it when it was never born in the first place? The separate individual with so-called free will is totally imaginary, a collection of feelings, thoughts, memories, and functionings superimposed upon pure living awareness. This collection of psychic imaginings, bewitching though they are, actually reduces

39

living awareness to a shadow of its true self. This misty shadow called a person also breaks loose with the destruction of the body. What remains is what we always have been—pure living consciousness. Free of all superimpositions and imaginings, we are now more alive than ever in love and beauty, home at last in our father's house. This great returning to the place I never left is not so much a journeying out and back, of being lost and being found; rather it is that we wake out of our sleep of earth, our dreamworld of many possible worlds where no one is born and no one dies—just a shady happening within the misty mansions of home.

BLUE PLANET LIVING

To live life aboard the blue spaceship we call Planet Earth is mostly always to travel second class. There is always something that could be better, even when we are having a pleasant trip. There somehow seems to be something missing. Life, we feel, just isn't first class, and happiness would somehow appear to be just around the corner. But if we never appear to get there, how do we know it exists? If it is always somewhere ahead of us, how can we miss or long for what we have never known? Is this a journey with no ending, always a journey and never a destination, or are we perhaps facing the wrong way? Maybe what we are searching for is behind us and not out ahead. What if we were to travel back through our outward experiences and start to revisit the already known. I would suggest that living first class is in fact a return trip to the splendid vision of something already known. In our funfair-like lives aboard Planet Earth, our heads and our hearts have been taken for a ride. We are dizzy and disorientated, bewitched and bewildered by the sleight of nature's hand. We get fostered out of mind and home, travelling, as Wordsworth proclaimed, "not in entire forgetfulness" and not in utter nakedness but "trailing clouds of glory do we come from God who is our home." If we could only entirely forget the glories we have known, then happiness and peace would be ours to take aboard our mysterious blue planet. Yet we can't entirely forget and we can't entirely remember. This is our dilemma and we struggle to make do with what we find and make the best of what comes our way.

> *Things are joined together by the boundaries we ordinarily take to separate them*
> ALAN WATTS

Supposing, though, the dusty clouds were to rise in the clear light of a fine day and afford to us a bright vision, perhaps the distant hills of our homeland might suddenly come into view.

There is, of course, another possibility. Maybe we never left our homeland in the first place. This is not to say that we haven't journeyed. We do it all the time. The fact is that our homeland has no boundaries and no frontiers, all lands are our lands, everywhere is ourwhere and everywhere is here. Time and eternity is forever, no time at all. We can only measure our lives in dreamtime and we dream our earthly lives in no time. When you and I stand across our separateness you see the greatest dreamer and I the greatest dream. The dream and the dreamer give birth to one another—one is the otherness of the other. The creator and created—the father and the son—all contained in the great mirror of awareness. Outside the divine mirror nothing is, nothing exists; all takes place within the magic glass. To look out from within the divine mirror we are looking from behind our eyes, not with our eyes, we see not with censorial looking, which is always suspect, but with uncensored intuition, which is not dependent on nor enhanced or impoverished by any outside influences or imaginings.

The immense magnitude of our great otherness stands like the slender thread of a spider's magical climbing rope. We may be totally unaware of its existence, and our conscious memory of past and present experiences may provide little or nothing in the way of evidence of its existence, and yet it is the mirror that makes all experiences possible.

HILLSIDE HAPPENINGS

The day Jim the Rock was walking the steep side of his mountain land, he felt very easy in himself. He was always happy to get a chance to rise above and away from life on the small farm he loved. Not that there was much happening to trouble him these days. Yet he still liked to rise above the narrow sloping valley where he was born and had lived all his life. He never married and, from listening to the married men he knew and would often take a drink with, he felt he had made the right decision. It somehow didn't seem right that a stranger could walk into your place and own half of it without ever having as much as lifted a hand to do a stroke of work on the place. To give half of everything you had to someone you hardly knew at all, sure you'd have to be soft in the head to do something like that. Anyway, Jim the Rock knew that he was too odd in his ways to share his time and table with anyone. His only sister, Bríd, had lived with him up to time she took the jump. It was a made match and

43

she married into the money and the land of her dreams. They were welcome to her, as far as Jim was concerned. It wasn't that Jim disliked Bríd; in fact he admired her greatly. She was a great girl, always willing to help out and she would never be found wanting when you needed her most. No, it was her attitude that he had most difficulty with; her constant complaining and negative outlook often drove him out of the house to seek solace in the outside world of no talking. He just could not understand how anyone could live like that. In Bríd's world being right and good amounted to the careful avoidance of actions that might give rise to pleasure, and her view of the future often resembled that of a person in the latter stages of a breakdown where O Sweet Misery was always waiting round the next corner.

Bríd was always giving out about the way Jim took life nice and easy. When she was mad at something, he would say "In this life we are only like a spark rising from the fire, that's all." This would incense Bríd all the more, so then he would try to console her by saying "You're right, Bríd, sure wouldn't something like that bring tears to a glass eye?"

She could never understand why Jim seldom got upset over the troubles of everyday life. "What kind of a future is ahead of us at all," she would often ask. "I suppose the Poor

House is what's facing the two of us the way you're carrying on, walking around the hills, staring off into space as if you were waiting for something to fall out of the sky."

"Ah, now, Bríd, sure God will take care of everything, you worry too much about things that never happen. You're always regretting the past and the mistakes you made. Why didn't I do this? Why didn't I do that? Sure, that's a sore carry-on altogether. The only time, Bríd, we can do anything about anything is right now today and that's it. Tomorrow will take care of itself and we will do the best we can and that's good enough." Jim knew she didn't understand; not many people did, but Jim knew and he had good reason to know after that day long ago sitting at Mike Dan's fireside. How could anything ever be the same again after that evening on the south side of the mountain?

Jim had known Mike Dan since he was a child. Often he would hear the old people talking and telling stories that even they themselves could scarcely believe, never mind understand. Many a person had sat by Mike Dan's fireside and found themselves pouring out all their troubles. Things that had never been told to anyone would all find the light of Mike's fire. People found it very strange indeed, because they would not have intended to speak of these deep secrets, old hurts and fears, but somehow it just happened once they started talking about themselves to Mike Dan. He wouldn't say much at all but there was something about his face, and especially his eyes, that made you feel relaxed and comfortable after only a short while in his company. He never spoke ill of or criticised anyone. Somehow you felt sure that whatever you told him would never be repeated.

Everyone was welcome at Mike Dan's cottage. They would come often just to be in his company for a while. He treated everyone the very same and somehow when you left you felt sure that he was your best friend and yours alone.

He loved books. They were everywhere to be seen, mostly stacked upon one another, rising from the old wooden floor. He never seemed to tidy up the house or put anything in its proper place, yet things were grand right where they were, with Mike sitting in the old chair made by his grandfather without ever using a nail or a screw. Wherever Mike Dan was, he looked easy in himself. Everyone loved to see him coming to their door, and even cross dogs found it hard to bark when he approached. He loved animals and humans alike and would greet both as if he was welcoming home a long lost brother or sister. Everything about him seemed to take place in slow motion, as though eternity had come to visit and decided to stay. One of his elderly neighbours who knew Mike Dan from the day he stepped from the cradle used to say that if Mike were to walk west towards the Atlantic, by the time he reached half way coastal erosion would have travelled the other half to meet him.

Jim the Rock had known for many years that there was much more to life than met the eye. He knew this in his heart and found making thoughts or words out of that knowing almost impossible. For instance, he felt sure that there was a flow to life and if we could only leave things alone, life would happen all by itself. He thought about that particular day he found himself standing outside Mike Dan's door. He never intended to go there that day. He had left the house early to walk the mountain because for some time he had had great trouble staying in the bed. It was a terrible thing when a man couldn't lie straight in his own bed. Bríd had gone and married the man of her dreams. He didn't mind being alone, it wasn't that, but he felt very restless and ill at ease with himself. Everything was a bother to him lately and there were times he felt like a briar. His eyes had seen fifty-five times the falling leaves of autumn, which seemed to come faster every year. Maybe he should have got married after all. God knows, he had chances enough— quite a few girls had set out their stall for him but they

47

always married someone else or went away working abroad. Whatever it was that ailed him, Jim felt sure a walk on the mountain would help clear his head. Mike Dan was still in bed when he heard Jim calling out "Are you dead or what, Mikeen? Will you get up out of that, for Christ's sake? It's no wonder the country isn't half settled, with people still in bed in the middle of the day." Mike was still laughing as he came down from the loft. "Welcome, Jim, welcome, Jim the Rock, you must have an awful bad bed to be out at this ungodly hour." Jim seated himself on one of the old fireside chairs. A few smouldering embers still kept life in the previous night's fire. Mike made tea; he was always drinking tea, good and strong was how he liked it with plenty sugar. "To keep the life in us," he would say.

Everything about that day was strange to Jim now. Whatever had happened, it had changed him and his way of looking at life for ever. He remembered sitting close to the fire opposite Mike Dan. He couldn't remember exactly what they had talked about, but at some stage in the conversation he felt he was talking but he couldn't hear himself; his lips were moving but there was no sound, and if there was sound he couldn't hear it, but he could well remember Mike Dan's eyes. Somehow he could not avert his gaze away from Mike's. A great easy feeling fell over him and he could re-

48

member no more, only standing up and suggesting to Mike that they go up the mountain for a walk. "Sure, it's too late now," Mike had said. "The night will be down on us soon." "What night?" said Jim. "It can't be night." When Jim looked at the clock Mike had below in the room, it was half past eight in the evening. "God Almighty, I better pull out before dark. God Bless you, Mike Dan." When Jim struck out for home he felt as if he were walking in a dream. He felt so at peace with himself. He could never remember feeling this good. His mind was so still and peaceful; all anxiety and fear had vanished. He wasn't even thinking how good he was feeling, he just was. That night he had the best sleep he ever had. He awoke in the morning feeling better still and began to recall the events of the previous day. Something had happened, yet he wasn't sure what exactly it was. It was good, he knew that. What he did not know was where the day had gone. Time had somehow disappeared into itself. He remembered the feeling of not hearing himself speaking and wondered how that could be. He remembered too how soft Mike Dan's voice was and that sometimes he only barely heard what he was saying. The old people were right after all: there was something not of this world about Mike Dan, and whatever it was it had now touched Jim the Rock to his very soul, and life would never be quite the same again.

Now as he settled himself gently into the dry heather high up on the mountain side, Jim thought back over his life and how he had changed almost without realising anything was happening. He was sure it had started that day with Mike Dan. He hadn't told anyone. How could he? Sure, people might only be talking and anyway it didn't seem right to broadcast something that was so personal and so open to misunderstanding.

He went back to Mike Dan's house many times after that and always came away with a few books. Reading was something he had done very little of since his school days. Now he was reading morning, noon, and night. A mighty hunger and thirst for more understanding of life's mysteries had come upon him. Nothing he had ever learned in school and in school books could satisfy him now.

Often he had wondered why in God's name this was happening at all, and what exactly we he looking for anyway? There were no easy answers, yet he knew Mike Dan would not have led him astray, and he never ever doubted anything Mike had said, even if he didn't always understand. Although his daily life remained very much the same, and there was always work of some kind to be done on a small hillside farm, Jim the Rock would find himself pondering, sometimes agonisingly, about something he had read. More often than not, it might concern the things Mike Dan had said. How he would love to sit down now with Mike and have a chat. He had discovered so much about the spiritual life from the books Mike gave him and he knew in his heart it was more than second-hand information. Jim had long since realised that there was a way of learning and discovering that went beyond all books and spoken words. Intuition, Mike Dan had called it. "When the time is right, Jim, you will know with all your heart, and there will be no doubting it whatsoever."

Mike Dan's death had rattled Jim despite all he had been told; somehow it just wasn't right for someone like Mike to die. He had helped so many people, young and old. They had all come and laid their troubles at this fireside. Men and women alike would bare their souls and be healed in his presence. "This cancer will kill the body, but I am not the body," Mike had told Jim who was stunned into silence at the bad news, "Remember there is no Mike Dan to die and no Jim to cry." He would never forget these words from his dying friend. Their true meaning had taken a long time to understand fully. It happened one evening as he was reading. He looked up from the book and suddenly, in an instant, he understood. Tears of joy rolled down his face.

51

He knew at last beyond all doubt, beyond all knowing, the truth of all Mike Dan had said. The sayings of Jesus, of the Buddha, and of all the great mystics that had been his constant companions for so long were all unveiled in one glorious moment. He now understood more in an instant than could be spoken of in a million lifetimes. How Mike Dan would laugh now and say "Sure, didn't I tell you? Life as we know it is like a tragic comedy. Remember, Jim, what Shakespeare said about life being 'a tale told by an idiot, full of sound and fury, signifying nothing'. You see, Jim, it is we as consciousness who create the world and all it contains including you and me. But we are not you and me, we are the stuff that all the yous and mes that ever lived and will ever life are made of. We are one, Jim, one with the father, one with all. Eternal life is not something we have, it's what we are."

They could have some mighty conversations now if Mike was still around, but then again maybe there was nothing more to be said.

GENTLY UPON THE EARTH

Perhaps it could be argued that as a species our attitudes and actions are often a disgrace to ourselves and to all of creation. There can hardly exist a greater hypocrisy than the pointing of the human finger at the so-called dumb animals and the consequential raising of ourselves to some imaginary higher standing. The fact that the evolutionary process has brought about the capacity for self-consciousness through thinking is partly responsible. Were it not for this peculiar human affliction and the resultant emergence of the imaginary thinking centre or ego, such disastrous behaviour might have been avoided. Again, to fully understand we must return to the beginning with an open and innocent mind. This may not be so easy, as the very thing we are investigating is in some way also doing the looking. Our old friend, the "me", must once again come under the microscope of our awareness. Let us firstly deal with the issue of awareness and the "me". Are they, for instance, two separate entities or are they one and the same thing? That I am aware goes without question. This awareness cannot be denied, otherwise I would surely be denying my own existence. I am aware, full stop. Now most of us would readily agree that "Yes, I am aware" and this is the very seed of the whole issue. Is there an "I" or a "me" that

53

is aware, or is there just awareness? This needs to be considered very carefully.

The horse stands in the field and knows that it is aware, that it exists. Like the other inhabitants of the so-called lowly caste we have consigned it to, it appears to stand in perfect peace. The man also stands in the field and is aware and knows that he exists. He does not, however, stand in perfect peace; if peace of any kind is experienced it is momentary and rarely if ever appears uninduced in modern man. So here we have two inhabitants of Planet Earth standing together and yet standing greatly apart. That both have intelligence is without doubt. That one has four legs and the other two is also obvious. Most of the other physical features are the same—two eyes, two ears, one mouth, one back, etc. There are some differences, of course, yet basically they are very similar. So what, if anything, really sets these two creatures apart? In the teachings of old, the difference hinged firmly upon the opinion that man had a soul, whatever that is, and the unfortunate animal did not. Of course, it did not end there. As the horse didn't possess a soul it could never go to heaven, wherever that was. Also it was not "fashioned in god's likeness" like us. What we can now deduce from this much-propagated teaching is that God doesn't look like a horse or any other animal for that matter. So why does the horse stand in perfect peace and the man in imperfect peace? There are a number of reasons:

(i) The horse is not aware that it is a horse, firstly because its method of communication does not require a symbol-laden structure like our language where everything needs to be named, classified, and pigeonholed into separate compartments. No, the horse has a much more streamlined and less cumbersome method of wordless communication through intuition, something we in our wisdom have consigned to secondary importance.

(ii) The horse is not aware of being a horse because no ego or imaginary thinking centre has been superimposed upon the pure awareness. The horse is conscious but not self-conscious. Here awareness and consciousness are one and the same. The awareness that animates the body and supports the life and intelligence system of the horse is pure awareness, pure life without any trace of a "me" whatsoever. Thus the horse stands gently upon the earth, at one with its surroundings and all that exists, including its rather strange two-legged companion.

(iii) With the non-existence of the "me" feeling and the non-emergence of the "I" reducing valve on pure awareness, there consequently exists no spatial isolation or feeling of other than me in the psychological sense for the horse because no division or separation between the "me" and the "not me" arises in its undivided mind. The feeling of being isolated and separated from all else never arises. Therefore it naturally follows that the concept of space as an isolating and empty distance between the horse and all that is not the horse does not take place.

(iv) Without the powerful and bewitching "me" feeling and without the ego, which is really only a feeling, the horse is free from all psychological fear, the prison warden of the man. Ego, by its very nature, is always in movement and because it has no place to lay its head, it is constantly in search of support and approval and new activities by which it can avoid fear.

(v) The relatively innocent process of thinking for the man gets prostituted into projecting and demanding a future— the so-called "unknown". The ego, which is now the slave-master of thought, stands desperately clinging to the known past for security. But the ghost-like ego feeling finds itself constantly standing on the dark precipice of the unknown future. Fear is therefore its constant companion. The thinking process is now held captive and forced into projecting a safe future to ensure the continuation and survival of the ego. Unlike the peaceful horse, the man can know no rest. The ego, now firmly established as the thinking centre, is constantly at war, and full alert is the order of the day. So they stand together sharing our nowhere planet. The man, blessed by his gods with an intellect, looks unhappily down on the horse from his lofty pedestal. Yet the horse stands free in blissful peace, free of thought and all that thought has mischievously created, fearing neither past nor future, remaining unhurried and unruffled by time present or otherwise. To live outside time, the horse simply remains as it is, neither being this nor that or anything in particular. Forever resting in the continuous now, its attention always focused

I felt through all this fleshy dress bright shadows of eternity

HENRY VAUGHAN

without any effort, it remains fully and absolutely alive to the ever-passing stream of events. The man also has the capacity for this lifestyle once the truth has been awakened in the intuitive intelligence he has in abundance. This intelligence goes far beyond the power of thought, which is by its nature restrictive and limited. To remain in this intelligence/awareness, the man, like the horse, has to do absolutely nothing because this is his eternal nature. From this standpoint the superficial distinguishing differences between the man and the horse fall away and now for the first time they stand together, undivided by anything and everything thought can create. The man at last can have true compassion for the person he takes himself to be and for all of living life. Understanding liberates, and liberation brings true freedom, and this truth has no opposite but encompasses and transcends all opposites. Now everything that thought has ever held falls into the truth and all differences are dissolved therein.

UNHEALTHY EGO

There is nothing solid or independent or unrelated, everything is created and connected by energy or spirit. If a tear falls to the ground in West Cork, Ireland, the mountains in Northern China vibrate. Everything can travel on this consciousness—like thought, which is a movement in consciousness. For example, two people can have the same thought or feeling at the same time even though they live thousands of miles apart. Of course, only the two bodies appear to be apart—the thing that is experiencing the feeling is consciousness looking out at the world through the eyes of the two separate bodies. There is only one consciousness, and many bodies of all different kinds and shapes. I can know all this at an intellectual level and say that it all makes good sense and say "now I understand", but the essence of this cannot be truly understood or known at the level of intellect; it can only truly be understood by our intuitive intelligence. Once we learn to trust our intuition, it comes into play more and more in our daily living; we begin to trust our feelings and are guided from a deeper level.

The mind is a wonderful instrument when used properly, but we live from our heads to an unhealthy degree and so live in a very partial way. Only when we begin to live from our hearts and our intuition can we start to live a more holistic life. When we live solely from the level of the intellect, we develop an unhealthy ego and lose the balance that is so important for a harmonious inner life. The unhealthy ego often assumes an exaggerated sense of self-importance, and unconsciously we become isolated and solely dependent on the mind for all the answers to life's problems. When all is well with us, this may work. When things start to go wrong, however, we may find ourselves eventually in great pain yet still believe that we can think our way out of our problems, and so become close-minded to any ideas but our own. We are unable to see anything wrong in our thinking or actions; we are in denial, we feel threatened, and are unconsciously afraid, so we become angry and defiant and more isolated than ever. We are totally at the mercy of the ego, which has now taken the sense of being a separate individual to a new and unrealistic level, compounding the isolation even further.

The whole situation is now out of hand, and outside help. The ego feels threatened like never before and clings on, desperately trying to remain in control. It struggles violently and now even suicide may seem attractive because it brings a feeling of power or control once more. The suicidal person very often appears in good form at this stage because the terrible conflict in the mind is over; a way out has been found and the ego is once more in control. Nobody must now be told about this, as that would give away the power and control. If the person does finally take their own life, it comes as a terrible shock, because the person seemed okay, and those close to the person may blame themselves for not realising that something was wrong. With this kind of suicide, the victim goes out of the way to give the impression that they are okay, because the ego must protect the feeling of power and control at all costs. This, of course, is just one aspect of suicide.

There is, however, one other possibility, which may not present itself. The mind or ego, finding no way out of the crisis, may just surrender and, with the right circumstances, accept or look for help. This is ego deflation at a profound level and leaves the person receptive to outside help or suggestions. Sometimes people in this position can experience a profound psychic change or spiritual experience that brings them to a full recovery, or at least to an acceptance of what troubles them, even if it means that there is to be no full recovery or no getting better. They may be faced with the fact that they are going to die or that there is no cure and no future in life. In this state of egolessness, they become one with the One, and the sense of separation and isolation collapses. But in truth we were always one with the One, or one with God or the self.

The feeling of being a separate individual arises only with the ego—I am this or that, or I am this and not that. Prior to this thought, which usually takes place around the age of two to three years old, there is just the feeling of being present, or just being. At that stage there is no duality or conflict and there is neither time nor space. We are not conscious of even having a body, all the actions of which happen naturally and spontaneously, like hunger, crying, going to the toilet, etc. With the beginning of thought and identification with the body, we start to take responsibility

61

for these natural events. Then comes the conditioning from our parents and the whole business of separation, isolation, and duality begins, and we fall from grace. From now on we leave our true home and father, identifying with name and form only, but we never quite forget that state of true bliss and love—and throughout our time in exile we are constantly trying to recapture our former glory and to strive for happiness in outer things, but unconsciously there is the sense of loss, of being incomplete right now but somehow it will be better in the future, and so we are always moving away from what we are trying to find, like the cat trying to catch its tail. We create a god far off somewhere, thus deepening the sense of isolation and imagined separation; we are living to all intents and purposes in hell. The ego is our devil, our jailer, and we its prisoners. For most of us, there is no parole or freedom unless the all-dividing me feeling is seen for what it really is, just another thought; then we remain what we have always been, pure awareness, pure consciousness, pure spirit, love and bliss, eternal life, complete in every way.

LIVING AND DYING

I often ponder what exactly it is about—life in human form that makes most people want to cling to life at all costs and makes some people want to end it all by whatever means lie at their disposal. As with nearly all aspects of nature and human behaviour, both the question and the answer are seldom cut and dried. This is always more evident when a tragedy takes place. Mostly our human minds want to wrap up all the loose concepts into neat little bundles that we can understand. This practice helps make us feel more secure and safe. But we are not safe regardless of how much wrapping up, rejecting, or discarding we furiously engage in.

Probably one of the most disturbing forms of death for most people is suicide. The very fact that someone might not want to preserve their life is an affront and a challenge to those who dislike even the notion of death. For those who enjoy life to the full and relish the challenge of a new tomorrow, suicide is absolutely incomprehensible. Medical advances have meant that staying alive was never easier. There are those who see death as a failure and feel guilty that more could not have been done after losing somebody they love or were acquainted with. This whole subject of life and death is of the most incredible importance to all of us who wish to live the best human life possible. Yet we mostly deal with life and death in a very hit and miss fashion. Probably what makes life unsafe for most of us is our refusal to face the facts outside of our preordained philosophies or religions, but having handy answers is a bit like speaking a foreign language out of a phrase book.

On a crisp November morning high in the southern mountains of Andalucia in southern Spain, the bright sun struggles lazily over the surrounding hill tops to warm the new day below on the valley floor. A small group of neighbours gathers by the dirt track roadside and stare at the lifeless body of a young man hanging from the front sun porch of a small house. The lifeless, almost childlike form was that of a talented sculptor who, when equipped with hammer and chisel, could encourage the stones to speak. Yet there his body hung like a worthless dishcloth on a clothes-line. The small assembled group tried to avert their gaze as much as possible while awaiting the arrival of the authorities.

Most of us would prefer not to have to come into contact with this kind of tragedy if possible, and yet to run away from death is to run in a useless circle, for to run from death of any kind is to run from ourselves. Also, running from death is running from life. In general, most societies have customised death, a preordained ritual to help us cope with the finality of this dramatic happening. For most cultures, the bluntness and uninvited intimacy of death is dealt with by various methods: the dressing up of the body in the best clothes of the deceased and in most instances the altering of facial features, which are all designed to make the corpse look as alive as possible. This, of course, may be taking place consciously or unconsciously. Whether or which, it is mostly done for the benefit of the living rather than being of some importance to the dead person. There is little need or use in making any visual or physical alterations for the dead person. He is dead and his body is of no further use and must be disposed of as quickly as possible. However, when we are brought face to face, unprepared and unforewarned, with the brutality of death, such as in the case of suicide or sudden death, we are immediately struck by the sheer vulnerability of living and the absolute uselessness of the human body once the vital life has been forced out of it. The body of the young sculptor hanging by the neck in the early morning sunshine brings this unavoidable fact home with a clarity and suddenness that is inescapable. If I spend my life believing that I am my body, and that your body is who you are, then it is right here that our major difficulty with death begins. From this standpoint onwards our very foundations are constructed of rice paper. This then is the flimsy safe place where we are psychically housed. From here we travel forth to do battle with disappearing life itself. At every hand's turn our original mistaken identity is cemented into living fact, but our living facts are strictly relative and owe their truth to uninvestigated assumptions and rumours.

How easily a life can be lived and accepted with honour as being the way it has to be. We place our collective shoulders to the wheel and push furiously up the slippery slopes of life where our joy is short lived and our efforts poorly rewarded. We fall back into dust as life's fast-moving wheel comes crashing downwards to destroy whatever stands in front of it.

Generation after generation gets swallowed up by the earth like some devouring monster that is never satisfied. Bodies of humans and all other creatures melt into dirt like winter leaves. "How is John keeping?" someone might ask. "Oh, he is dead and buried," comes the reply. Now is John dead? What exactly is it that has died? Was the body that was buried really John? Was there someone called John living inside that body and, if so, where is he now? Is he also dead? Was there ever a John born in the first place and, if so, when did he enter the body? We know that the body had its beginnings when the vital fluids of the two parents came together. Did this John exist before this merging or was it after as the shapeless speck of matter began to take shape as an infant. Here, another important question presents itself. What exactly was doing the growing? What power or life force was present and when did it enter the equation—when the two vital fluids merged together, or was it present in both separately before conception? We can talk about genetics and biology all we like but the questions we are asking do not concern these. We were endeavouring to establish if John was now dead and gone. Here our investigation centres on when and how John entered the equation in the first place. Did this person John wish to be born and develop into the exact person he was? Did his parents choose that particular baby with all the various characteristics of personality and body that they called John? Were they in any way responsible for the development of John from a shapeless particle of matter to an infant child who emerged nine months later?

The fear of death is the fine for accepting the identity of the body as a separate entity

NISARGADATTA

So who has been born before name, nationality, and all the

67

other conditioning factors have been added? A small body has emerged after passing through other bodies. These bodies are the expression of nature's hand and dependent upon that hand for survival and are deeply entwined with the earth upon which they stand. This newly born infant, who in truth does not belong to any one person or persons, lies complete and secure, cocooned in the womb of oneness, untouched by divisions or separation, oblivious to any labels that are soon to be imposed upon its head. The pair of adult humans our language terms as parents are in fact two strangers who are in most cases unrelated by blood. So too were the so-called parents of these parents. The infant later to be labelled John will have genetically inherited various characteristics from a long line of total strangers who in all fairness cannot claim direct or sole ownership to any particular individual.

A perfectly natural event has taken place. In this instance, it concerns the human animal. However, it could just as well have been a happening involving almost any other species; birthing in the human sense is no different from all others. John comes equipped with happiness complete, needing nothing or anything that might suggest that he was in any way especially different from any of the other gifts that nature gives to itself. However, things soon start to take a particularly human turn. Firstly, John's parents, unlike other species, are self-conscious or ego-conscious and, as far as they are concerned, this is their doing alone and this is their baby and theirs alone. The first thing to be done is to stick a label of their choosing on this gift of the universe. The person, John, is born. A universal happening now becomes personalised as the parents take sole ownership and all responsibility—a conscious contract that may last the rest of their lives. John, of course, is blissfully unaware of any such contract or personalisation and, once his basic needs are provided, he couldn't care less. This is innocence and love, untainted with the burden of self-consciousness. It radiates in peaceful splendour to warm our sorely neglected adult hearts. Unfortunately, and all too soon, the veil of our inherited conditioning will be drawn in all innocence and without any intentional wrong-doing across nature's magnificent handiwork. Our infant child sets off on a life's journey in the vehicle of the human body.

The blunt instruments of words and symbols fall heavily on the heads of our children and our gods. Words like John, person, parents, life, or death create nothing in truth. They were not prior to any event that takes place. These symbols serve only to describe or distort what already is. That there might be a truth or a reality that cannot be held or in any

69

way adequately described by our words and language makes us feel greatly uncomfortable and inadequate in ourselves. Our first reaction is to reject and denounce that which we fail to reduce sufficiently to the realm of our learning and treasured intellect. Only when our intuition, which is our spiritual intelligence, is awakened from its enforced slumber are we able for the greater truths of life, the very building blocks of eternity and our one self.

Long before his physical birth, John was aware and knew that he existed. This brings us to the mother of all questions: where did this awareness or consciousness come from? We have already established that, without it, the body is useless and non-functional. Was this awareness born also, or was it somehow prior to the emergence of the physical components that make up the human body? When the child John looked out upon the world, what exactly was doing the looking? The eyes in themselves see nothing as, like the rest of the body including the brain, they are simply instruments. The answer must surely lie further back along the chain of events, or maybe we might be brave enough and unscientific enough to suppose that this conscious awareness somehow existed before the miracle of the physical took place. It is important to remember that our investigation here includes all earthly life and not just the human being. When we look with a cold eye we will see that human conception and birth are not in any way greater or more special than the miracle of the many other forms of life. Take, for instance, all the other beings with whom we share our planet: there are animal beings, bird beings, fish beings, all arriving equipped with their own natural intelligence. The question that now presents itself is: when exactly did the vital life force first enter into the equation? Our often-asked question whether the chicken or the egg came first is simply the wrong question, and one that will inevitably bring the wrong answer. The real question must be: what was it that, prior to the egg and the chicken, provided the all-important spark of life? Only the discovery of what was prior to the emergence of matter can surely provide the answer, because neither the egg nor the chicken were primary, as they could not have emerged out of nothing.

Perhaps our investigation has now arrived at a crossroads or a roundabout that demands we wheel the telescope around one hundred and eighty degrees, where we find ourselves once again under the spotlight of our own questioning. If the spirit of awareness was somehow present before the vital fluids of John's parents made contact with one another, would it be fair to assume that the awareness we call John was present before the body he later, mistakenly, thought was himself came to be? This awareness spirit is therefore not dependent on any physical body for its existence. That being the case, when the body breaks down and stops working as in death, the life awareness remains unaffected and undisturbed. Where does the awareness go when the body dies? The answer, speaking absolutely, is nowhere. It cannot go anywhere because it is everywhere already. It cannot return to anywhere because it never left. It cannot merge with anything when there is nothing but itself everywhere. Every apparent separation or isolation is simply a transparent veil, majestically and artistically thrown across our god reality by a scintillating array of sensory equipment. Now add to these earthly building blocks another special effect of consciousness at large, namely personalised self-consciousness, then stir gently with loving care, slowly adding a light sprinkling of mind conditioning (name, age, nationality, etc.). Then add some time and a little space and the self-raising ingredients of language and symbolism. Then place the whole concoction in the heat of parental love and longing. What emerges out of the womb of expectant society is an imaginary individual called John whose reality is strictly relative to all that he is taken to be.

NOT INVOLVED

We love being human and we love being itself, and sometimes we find it hard to separate one from the other. Perhaps for most of us the notion of any difference at all has never really concerned us. The idea of retaining our sense of being without being one thing or another seems very strange indeed—it's just so hard to imagine being bodyless. This is due mainly to our misplaced sense of identity with our bodies. If I am not something in particular then surely I am nothing—no thing, emptiness. Because I have accepted myself as being just one small thing—a human body—it is impossible to imagine being somehow bigger or greater than the particular. The notion that somehow I will remain alive even after the death of my body and be fully aware, more aware than ever before, seems to be almost beyond comprehension. Without a body, brain, eyes, and all the other bits of equipment, just how am I going to be so aware? I cannot be touched, heard, seen, or known in any way, shape, or form. I will be neither this nor that, not absence or presence, not the absence of presence nor the presence of absence. Nothing can describe what I will be after the death of my body. So what? That's not so strange because nothing can describe what I am now. Right now, what am I? All the words I might use to describe what I am mean absolutely nothing. They are just sounds, noises, nothing. You see, we create a reality out of words and language which is nothing. Language creates only a symbolic reality that either describes or distorts what we interpret as real. The fact remains that it is a useless exercise to try and understand what we call the afterlife until I first understand what I am in this life. The same goes for God: I want to know and understand God but I do not know myself. To make any kind of serious investigation we must first find out who the investigator is—just who it is that wants to know. We might, of course, have a belief about the afterlife or about God, but a belief, no matter how faithful or sure, is not an open-minded way of looking and may not bear any resemblance to the truth. We love to love and we love to live. We take ourselves to be the separate enjoyer of these sacred gifts, and this is the crux of our dilemma. We seem happy to settle for the action replay and almost always miss the real action. The reason I love to live is because I am life itself. It's my nature to live, I have always lived, and always loved eternally. Speaking absolutely, there is no reason for life as we experience it; like a wave rising on the surface of the ocean, it just is. The wave may sometimes appear to have a separate existence of its own but really it's all just the same water. The wave could not exist without the ocean. Let us take our inquiry a step further. Is the water in the wave different in any way from the water in the ocean? In other words, does the wave have a life of its own, separate from all else? Could it exist without the ocean? Is there one life force for the wave and another for the ocean? Is the ocean somehow wetter than the wave? The answer is surely no to all of the above, just as with life.

What we generally call reality is at best a description. All we can ever have at any one time is a description. It can never be any more real or unreal than that. When we attempt to construct a solid reality out of thought we do ourselves a grave injustice in the search for the truth. It is only by seeing the bigger picture that we might begin to understand the secret of life, and never by reducing it to a mental level. It is at this point that we generally feel an uneasy resistance from our ego to any interference with our cherished view of what's out there or in here. As we have previously seen, the ego is an abstract mental picture of ourselves, our own self-image or sense of self and the cause of all our woes. The very nature of the ego is resistance to change, including the fear of death and, in its flight from death, it reduces life or our idea of life to an opinion, dividing and separating on a mental level our true greatness and forcing us to live an impoverished life wedged in between past and future. Birth and death force us to identify with our bodies and minds and so miss the big picture. Our ego is the censor that cuts out all the parts of the picture it doesn't like and compels us to live with what is left. What's left is an illusion, just a patch of our former selves. What we have here is a ghost creating an illusion. Remember that what we call ego is, in reality, merely a feeling. We identify ourselves with this sense or feeling and ignore our total selves, our awareness, which is what we really are. We settle for our personality as being who we are and we wrongly accept that the thinking centre is me, that we are somewhere inside our heads doing the thinking so that the skin boundary becomes a prison in which we then live with a very narrow view of who we are, living in spiritual and emotional poverty and in a wrong relationship with others, the world about us, and ourselves.

Once the original identification with the ego, the me, has taken place, the dividing and separating never stops because whenever we draw a line it automatically becomes a battle line. Of course, there is nothing fundamentally wrong with the ego arising in the first place. That is not the problem; the problem is that I take it to be me—this is the original sin where the one gives birth to a second. The one is then discarded and the second becomes the one. It's a bit like taking a copy of a picture to be the original. But what if I could somehow remain in my true state as awareness? What then? Or is this too much to ask for? Well, not really. I am aware right now. I have always been aware. In fact, I am this awareness. From this standpoint of awareness I am aware of everything. I am aware of thoughts arising very rapidly one after another. I am also aware of thinking taking place—no need for a thinker, just thinking. All this happens automatically and spontaneously. I am also aware of feelings and body sensations arising with the thoughts; these too come up automatically and after a few moments pass away if I just watch them and do not react or get involved and remain as the witnessing awareness. I am aware of the body but I am not the body. I am aware of all the body's sensations, needs and

To be free from the idea of being someone, that is illumination

JEAN KLEIN

demands, but I am the awareness, just watching uninvolved the way I would watch others. I watch and hear speaking and I am aware. I am also aware of listening, there is no me listening, just listening, just observing, just being. It is an established fact that I can have only one thought at a time; thoughts arise at an incredible speed but I can never have two thoughts at the same time yet I am aware of my thoughts as they happen. This simple exercise proves that there is something about me that is, as John Moriarty says, "not involved", but is always very much present. The moment I become open to this way of looking, the more I begin to reside there and at last start to view the bigger picture. This awareness is not something I have like I have thoughts, emotions, or feelings. It is not an attribute of any kind. Awareness is the background of all that is; like the cinema screen it makes everything else possible but is itself dependent on nothing, and this is what I am and always have been. I look out through the eye but I am not the eye. An eye by itself sees nothing. I take myself to be in the body, yet it is the body that is within me. I think I am in the world but it is the world that is in me. I am there before it arrives. I am also there when it has left; everything has its being because I am. I am in everything and everything is in me. People will say I am crazy but I am also the people, so join the club—membership is for eternity.

WORSHIPPING FALSE GODS

There are no words that can adequately describe the mystic experience. Every word that is spoken about it takes away from what is experienced, reducing it to the rational level, the level of thought, which represents the divided mind. What is beyond thought can never be held by thought, so the mystics of all ages have used words in such a way that their essence and not the words themselves might carry the reader or listener closer to the experience. Words and all other symbols can only point to the fact, they can't create it, they either describe or distort the fact. Unfortunately, in most cases the words have been taken as facts, as the truth. The words have been preached but their essence has been lost or just not realised, and so we find ourselves in the sad position of worshipping another false god.

The truth can never be held in any way, it can only be experienced. But man has taken words to be the word of God; they are not. Words are very poor symbols, very restrictive; the word of God is a knowing with the whole mind, a realisation with our intuitive intelligence, which we have in abundance and which is not dependent upon the mind or thought for its existence. It comes into being when the mind is still, when we come to the end of our thinking. This can come about in different ways, by repetitive prayer, meditation, or direct inquiry. We live to all intents and purposes in a world of words. We view with suspicion anything that does not fit into our ideal world of words. However, the story is only a messenger, the servant, and not the master, not the truth.

In our world of appearances we glorify the individual, the person, and in so doing create a division where formerly there was none. We set ourselves apart from God. We see God as spirit and ourselves as bodies and persons. We are not. We too are spirit and truth. We appear to be separate from one another, from God, but we are not. There is only one of us, and no second. We may see ourselves as separate, like the pegs on a clothes-line, but in truth we are the clothes-line. Just as the line supports the pegs, we as spirit support our bodies and all else that exists in this world and all other worlds. If I look out to sea I see islands with different shapes, some big, some small. On the surface they are all separate but if I dive right down I find they are all connected by the ocean floor. They are not individual islands at all, they just appear to be, like you and I. In truth, we are one as consciousness. We live in fear of death yet what we really are was never born. Our sense of being present is wrongly attributed to the body. We imagine that without the brain we cannot be aware or conscious. In fact, it is the other way around; without consciousness the brain cannot function. When we say that a person is not conscious or unconscious, it is not consciousness that is absent, it is a breakdown in some of the physical body parts like the brain. When the body breaks down and the heart stops working, the body dies and what is known as an individual—which is imaginary and has no independent existence apart from the body-mind construct—also disappears, never again to be reborn. Self-consciousness also disappears and only consciousness remains as pure consciousness or awareness, pure subjectivity. This is what we are, have always been and will always be, totally unaffected by the appearance of bodies, people or any other apparent objects that exist in our wonderful world of appearances. The world is real enough; what is unreal is the way we look at it. Relatively, people and the world exist and are real. Absolutely, the world and people are appearances in consciousness. The world and the body that you take yourself to be are within you as consciousness or awareness or spirit or God, or any other name you wish to give it. What you are is not affected by the events that happen during a lifetime, and this consciousness is the background of everything, the source of all living things and all living worlds.

YOU ARE SAFER THAN YOU THINK

How strange it is that we know so much about our physical world and yet we don't know the knower. We never ask by what power we can feel and think. What is it that enables me to know that I know, and who is it that knows the knower? We are mostly content with our own make-believe world and our make-believe god. We make the best of what we have, what we know, think, and experience with our five senses and the power of thought. There are people who seem quite content with their lot and those who are not, who feel afraid, vulnerable, and discontent, seeking answers while wondering if this is all there is to life. We give them still more words, whether in the shape of a belief system or some philosophy, and they still feel lost and alone in a harsh and unforgiving world as they see it. It is to those people that this subject may be of most interest; it is to those who seek even though they know not what, who feel that there must be more to life, that this writing may give up its essence. The writing itself is just so many words but what it contains is beyond all words, symbols and thought, and beyond all that you will ever know, because you can't know what you truly are, you can only be it. In truth, there is nothing to be done and no-one to do it. Just be, you are safer than you think—all is well and all is very well.

ORDINARY OR EXTRAORDINARY?

Familiarity, it is said, breeds contempt. In what follows we will try to establish why this is so. Also, why is it that it generally takes an exceptional occurrence, something so out of the ordinary, before we declare it to be miraculous? And are these happenings really out of the ordinary, or is our ordinariness way out of touch with reality?

Perhaps our idea of ordinariness is just an idea, some kind of gentleman's agreement as to how things are and should be. Maybe this concept in our heads is nothing more than a framework of reference we superimpose upon our environment and life. The familiar, of course, has many advantages whether it be on main street, the family home, or indeed within the mind of the individual. But this need not concern us here. The challenge we are facing is, how does the familiar reduce our every-moment miracle of existence to the mundane. Does familiarity in helping us to feel so normal sometimes drive us to the point of distraction, where the heavy presence of our cherished familiar induces the feeling of losing our minds, so much so that for some one more day of normality is just one day too much, and they feel compelled to abandon ship?

Perhaps familiarity is a kind of mental illness with a narrow spectrum, a feeling of being safe in prison that renders all that lies outside it as being somehow alien. What we eventually end up with is a home-made version of the real thing which we proudly proclaim is the real world, when in fact what we see is a strictly relative head-given world, Our hand-made, home-made, head-made reality is nothing more than some Jack Nicholson-like creation ever striving towards goodness while at the same time unable to resist giving the devil more than his due.

When our flattering heads take us waltzing through life we forget our birth-given stupendousness and we are whisked off our feet by old twinkle toes himself. How shockingly easy we are led into forgetfulness by the ordinariness of life, which in spite of our forgetfulness is uncommonly awe-inspiring, and every moment miraculous. What we experience at any given time is what our heads allow us to experience, which in the swish of a horse's tail is processed, gift-wrapped and presented to consciousness as the agreeable and the acceptable because that's how egos work. Having it any other way tends to make us feel uncomfortable and insecure. "I prefer the usual please, thank you very much," the ego says. "I will try something new another time."

84

The shocking thing about the outrageously unexpected miraculous is that it lovingly trips the switch from the head to the heart where we are reminded of the former glory we had unconsciously forgotten to remember. As John Moriarty wrote, "Forgetting isn't forever."

Perhaps what we call miracles are the universe's way of administering a sort of electroshock treatment to the collective consciousness in the hope of shaking us out of our Ray-ban shaded sensory perceptions and restoring us to our childhood, supernatural way of being. Maybe then our poor overly intellectualised heads might lose their stumbling sadness, where on each waking into morning brightness we wake into our eternal miracle of existence, the shockingly ordinary miraculous.

THE WAY WE ARE

The way in which we collectively view death is in need of a radical overhaul. Death can arrive at our door in many different ways. It may be the result of many years of wear and tear, where the body simply breaks down and is beyond repair and unable to support the life force, or maybe it has come under attack from one of the many life-threatening diseases that medical science is still struggling with. Whatever the reason, being alive is still a very dangerous business. The human body is a remarkably robust piece of equipment which can often survive the most horrendous trials and yet, in almost total contradiction to this, it has an inbuilt vulnerability and fragility so life threatening that we mostly prefer not to contemplate it. Where that vulnerability mainly lies is in those aspects of the body over which we have absolutely no control, such as the heart, for instance. This muscular blood pump is completely independent of any human wishes, desires, or imagined will power, pumping a constant blood supply to all parts of the body—parts that operate collectively and individually without the slightest concern for the so-called me. In fact, the body as an instrument mostly shows a blissful indifference to all the many ideas and concepts I may hold about how it should behave. Powerlessness once again confronts us when we begin to look beyond what we have normally taken ourselves to be.

One of the most disturbing ways of death is suicide, disturbing that is for the relatives, loved ones, and friends of the one who is now dead. To anyone who has never walked down that narrow and usually one-way path, death by suicide is incomprehensible—it just doesn't seem normal, we feel, to take one's own life, to choose death over life. To die

86

in preference to living a life at all costs interferes shockingly with how we view the norm.

Of course, our idea of normality is not an absolute but is strictly relative to a particular time or situation. For instance, I may behave perfectly normally in the eyes of society at one time, and the same behaviour may be totally unacceptable at another time, even in a similar situation. The so-called normal simply does not exist. We mostly use terms like normal, proper, right, etc. to reduce the totality of daily happenings to a level we can more easily comprehend and be comfortable with. How easily we construct our concrete social norms and by doing so create a playing field that for some is a relatively pleasant

If God made us in his image, we have certainly returned the compliment
VOLTAIRE

and comforting challenge, while for many others it represents an arduous assault course which may bring with it a host of negative and destructive emotions that proceed to isolate, torture, and imprison. The resulting emotional pain reduces life and living to the hellish realms of the unacceptable and unbearable. This intensely private black world of emotional quicksand throws up for many just one alterna-

87

tive: to put an end to the pain by destroying totally the very instrument of feeling and sensation, the body-mind. This reaction to society's often insensitive and uninclusive norms may be the only option the suffering person feels he or she is left with. Reaching this decision in their private and powerless reality may often represent a tremendous sense of relief, providing at last a way out of a hell over which they previously had no control. Empowered now by the ability to reach a decision, they feel once again they have gained control of the previously uncontrollable. The suicidal person may feel they must not give away their new-found power of decision by telling anyone of their break for freedom, as they see it.

We would be well served here to remember that we are discussing just one aspect of suicide, and we would be foolish to try and simplify what is a minefield of ifs, buts and maybes. Perhaps our collective and individual responsibility rests in attempting to create a society in which all persons are awarded inclusivity. This should not be interpreted as equality, as this is an entirely different matter deserving a more thorough treatment than can be afforded here, except to state that to envisage equality is to aspire to another norm under which all might feel equal. Surely this societal structuring is precisely what we hope to escape from. All people are not equal as we generally understand the term and neither should they be. What is much more important is to recognise that all persons are different to one another, and although there certainly are similarities these are mostly superficial, even in identical twins. It is only when our societal groupings give due respect to our birthright of uniqueness and ensure as far as possible that individuality and not some new achievement is held most sacred that all persons will feel inclusively important and also feel that it is perfectly acceptable to be just the way they are. When engaging with someone who, for one reason or another, is experiencing great difficulty in coping with life, if I encourage or coerce them to act, think, or behave in a certain way, then I am a million miles away from where they stand. I am unintentionally concretising the painful notion that they are stuck in one place and the rest of society is further out ahead. I am reinforcing a normal and a not-normal, a right versus wrong. Only when I listen unconditionally to their pain, and I am standing in good acceptance of the contradictions in my own life, can I allow an atmosphere to develop, which suggests that whatever way they feel is perfect for right now. In this way normal and not-normal collapse into the present fact and cease to present themselves as the good and right versus the unthinkable and unimaginable. Thus the painful isolation that society and they themselves have notionalised themselves into is no longer the wrong place to be. In fact, now there is no other place. There is nothing wrong whatever with the way they feel right now, and whatever way that happens to be becomes free from the often mortally wounding inner conflict that freezes the individual into a mental hell where it seems that all doors are closed against them. In any worthwhile attempt to understand the darknesses of the psychologically troubled, I am obliged in all honesty to open myself generously to all that is darkness in myself. Any attempt to look down from some one-sided standpoint of self-perfection is guaranteed to produce only a partial and lopsided view of all I wish to understand. If I live lopsidedly, either denying or in blissful ignorance of all that is darkness and troubling in me, I am likely to unconsciously project all that I deny and fear onto the other person and then dislike it in them. Thus our difficulty in understanding another person's behaviour is often brought about by our refusal to look and accept all that might be unacceptable in ourselves. Acceptance, understanding, and allowing ourselves to be vulnerable bring about a spirit of loving awareness where the answers to our often profoundly troubling human conditions can present themselves, unsought and unstruggled for.

How stunningly different our everyday life would be if what once lay in the distant realms of the unfathomable and the almost unthinkable now became part of the everyday facts of life—simple truths our children and their children would be initiated into, magical bed-time stories not about make-believe wonderful worlds, but simply about the more than magical world of life on Planet Earth. What was formerly out of the question might now become the answer; the unknown has become the known and the knowable. The mental chasm that previously brought us to the end of our thinking and imagination now shows itself for what it truly is, not a chasm at all but a bridge.

Free at last from the indoctrination of the centuries, the truth and love that we have always been is not now something to be strived for by one practice or another—like one day I will find the truth and one day I will be able to love. Or only when I practice some discipline taught by some authority will I know love—or I will give up sex for the love of God, or I will give up all material possessions and purify myself. Of course, the tragic fact is that all of these ideas and theologies take us further away from love and truth, imprisoning us more than ever in our troubled heads and in into all the sadness, fears, regrets, and jealousies we become so wrapped up in. Every step the me takes to become more special is another step along the prison hallway. You see, every movement of the me is an expression of the fretful ego which is like a knot in consciousness and a restriction—bewitchingly real, yes, but still only a sleight of consciousness with no independent reality beyond the realms of thought. Now it is possible to look at all of this without the me, without the narrowness and the pettiness of the me and mine—my husband, my wife, my children, my country, myself. This surely is the question of all questions because if the answer is no, we are forever to be confined to the mundane with the odd fleeting pleasure sandwiched between the good and the not so bad. Is this then all there is? Must our high notions always finish up on the scrap heap of the ordinary where only the security of some outside authority offers a watered-down taste of home? If, however, the answer is yes, how then do we go about finding whatever it is that lies beyond all the pitfalls of the above? Perhaps the starting place lies in recognising exactly that the me and the mine are creations of a superficial reality. Unless this sorry state of affairs is challenged and inquired into, the road to freedom will lie always over some other hill.

When John Moriarty tells us that the mind is not the window to the soul but simply the blind, we should sit up and take notice, for here surely is the answer to our problems. But how are we to draw back the blind to the light of eternal life? Just how is it to be done? The answer is surely that it cannot be done because to do so requires a doer; to strive for the answer requires someone to strive, and the doer and the striver are of the mind, but if the mind is the blind then we are stumbling about in dark, misty circles, having the feeling we are getting somewhere yet always winding up back where we started.

Now if the mind is the blind then surely the mind is the problem. So what is mind anyway? For most people mind and brain are one and the same thing, and both are somehow connected to consciousness, whatever that is, and we generally accept that our brain does the thinking and remembering—all this somehow going on in our heads, that round ball on the top of our necks. Every challenge that presents itself in life only really becomes a challenge if I am willing to accept the uncomfortable feeling of being challenged. Am I willing to challenge my own accrued myths and beliefs, because this is surely what any genuine inquiry is all about. Now maybe, for instance, the brain is not where all the answers are to be found and maybe it is not where all the questions begin. This wondrous thing called the brain may be nothing more than an instrument. These are huge questions and ponderings and it may be much easier to walk away in the direction of the familiar than to turn our face towards the rocky road of the unknown. Perhaps only

93

those who find themselves at the crossroads of no choice can somehow summons the willingness to face the challenge of facing themselves.

Let's suppose for now that the brain is only an instrument, the microchip wonder of mother nature, the original prototype of present-day computerisation. This fleshy computer has evolved and is evolving through the centuries—invented, patented and presented by the hand that rocks the cosmic cradle. Spell-binding and wondrous for sure, but on deeper investigation even greater treasures come to light and the brain takes on a more reduced and instrumental role. The next question that presents itself is this: is there something that the brain is dependent upon and without which it is rendered useless? Surely it must be consciousness. So if the brain is dependent on this conscious life force for its functioning, where did consciousness come from? Most certainly it is not produced in the brain or by the brain, so it would naturally follow that this consciousness was prior to the development and existence of the brain. This being the case, and there is no evidence to say otherwise, then consciousness plays a more important role than our cherished brain, and perhaps even more than our poor heads are capable of understanding.

CHILDLIKE LOVE

When a child asks "What colour is the wind?" we should at least try to lend him a loving ear because maybe the answer to his question is also the answer to our aching hearts. Maybe it only takes a little signpost from the mind of a child to point us in the right direction on life's adventurous inner journey. This can only take place if what is inside our heads is less than what is outside; only when we are poor in our heads can we inherit this innocence. There is no point in taking a solid bucket to the well because the value of the bucket lies in the part that is not there. If the meek can inherit the earth, then maybe we too have a chance to claim our inheritance. Just look around you today and you will see that you are surrounded by meekness. The little child standing by your knee is meekness itself. The animals, the flowers, and all the unthinking organisms that surround us on all sides bring us this great gift, if only we are open to receive. If we pick out the fastest racehorse, the most valuable we can find, and look into its eyes, what do we see? Nothing, just emptiness. But it is not emptiness as we know emptiness. Those eyes are full of meekness and love because there is nobody who looks out—there is just looking. We might have a hard time trying to achieve what the horse has in abundance without doing anything. But seeing as the journey to God is a short one, we might not have too far to go. The child will, if we let him, take us by the hand and guide us in the way of the short cut. All we have to do is to walk as the child walks, stand as the tree stands, and run as the horse runs. Try to forget everything anyone has ever told us and just be—be still and know that I am God; be still and know that we are God.

The child, the horse, and the tree stand gently upon the earth, cocooned in the oneness of all things, as in the younger days of Thomas Traherne who noticed that "All things abided eternally as they were in their proper places. Eternity was manifest in the light of day and something infinite behind everything appeared, which talked with my expectations and moved my desires." When we extend our heart and hand in friendship and greeting to the child, our love is in full flower, because love is what we really are, and its expression is what we deny ourselves the most. Our thinking is the balaclava that conceals our true identity, and what we think we are is the deadly weapon we take to war with ourselves and all we consider to be not ourselves. One is because of the other. Eliminate one and the other disappears; what is left is what has always been—peace, love, God, you, me, and the world.

96

SPIRITUAL PIONEERS

The journey to God or the self is a journey that is both inward and outward, and takes place through a pathless land. We need not be afraid of this; although we may seem to walk alone, an unseen guide is always at hand, a guide who has already made the journey as a pathfinder into the unknown. Every age and culture has produced such spiritual pioneers, men and women who have earned the title of prophet, saint, or seer—Christ, the Buddha, St Paul, the Hindu and Muslim mystics of the East. In India, the Ramana Maharshi lived in a cave and never left it. Sri Nisargadatta raised a small family and lived in a small flat in Bombay. In Spain, St John of the Cross worked tirelessly to bring others his visions of the unknown. Among his students was St Teresa of Avila.

What these great spiritual guides show us is that taking a leap of faith and free-falling to God is also to free-fall to ourselves, to come to know our greater selves. If the kingdom of God is within us, we have to be more than just persons since being a person, an individual, is only a part of what we are. To reach our full potential, to live fully in love with ourselves and others, we might first become willing to trust the guides from outside, and they will point us to the great guide within. This is the greatest guide of all; once discovered, it will never leave us because it is part of what we are. But it can be obscured and shrouded from us by all that goes on in our heads. And as wonderful as our heads are, they are not all there is. God is not found in our thinking but in those almost imperceptible gaps between our thoughts, which provide an opening to the pathless land of home.

Asking that age-old question of ourselves, "Who am I?", with complete abandonment and sincerity is to invite into our lives a guide who may take many forms and who will point out to us all that we are not. When we accept all the things we are not, what's left is what we are, although we cannot know what we truly are; we can only be it. There is no need to be afraid; all is well, all is very well. We are already free, already home, we just don't realise it.

Almost all our psychological sufferings spring from the fact that we live a small life, in so much as we take ourselves to be much less than we really are; we live in a poverty that reduces us to mortal beings, squeezed between birth and death in an existence full of insecurities and boundary-building and where life itself is almost seen as a threat. We can talk of loving one another and the brotherhood of man, but the truth is that we are in competition with one another and there are boundaries between us of which we are not even aware. Our sense of love can vary between selfishness—"what makes me feel good"—to an unlimited array of security-seeking motives and actions which help to bolster our impoverished view of ourselves and further suppress our primal fear of death and the unknown. All this in itself would be bad enough, but it gets worse! Because we are drawn away from discovering the true magnitude of our limitless loveliness, we are also denied the chance to allow full expression to the love that we are. If the fragrance of a rose is a rose in prayer, then love in expression is love in prayer and this love is unconditional and without any need of reward.

> *I think continually of those who were truly great, who from the womb remembered the soul's history through corridors of light*
> STEPHEN SPENDER

When we begin to see that our idea of ourselves is basically flawed, we have at least found a place to start looking from. We should not have to experience some major crisis before we are able to discuss in an open-minded way this whole subject of you, me, God, and the world. I would like to think that most of the great religions of the world would

99

have started out in this innocent, welcoming manner. In Christianity, for instance, there is something lovely about the image of Jesus sitting by the side of the road talking to a group of people and encouraging them to look at themselves—and the dialogue that would have taken place, just a conversation by the side of the road. Afterwards the people would have gone about their business and maybe later in the evening they would have continued the discussion between themselves. Sadly, we seem to be missing the innocent space and humility that would allow us to discuss these things and feel that it's okay to say "I don't know."

We expect scientists or our religious leaders to have the answers for us, or we worship intellect as being the all-knowing and only means of giving us the answers. We live to a great extent in a very lopsided manner, living from our heads as we cling to the power of thought as if it were the only saviour we could trust. We squeeze our intuition and the feelings of our hearts into a miniscule part of our conscious life. We follow the "goose that lays the golden egg" of progress. But eggs can break and if the grey fox of life should take our goose, our gods of intellect are seen for what they really are—superficial structures and special effects that may not stand the test of time. If you and I can sit down together and speak about how we really feel without any judgment or looking for answers, just listening without trying to change one another, maybe then the innocent space we had in abundance as children can emerge once again. Our bashful emotions can start to emerge from the shadows, we can both walk together to a clearing in the woods where the sun shines over the top of our lofty intellects and maybe we can sit in peace unhindered by our mental boundaries. Maybe we are in trouble whether we realise it or not or maybe we are afraid to admit it to ourselves and unable to admit it to others. We so much need that warm, safe clearing where we can step out of time and rediscover the gentle innocence of compassion and listening. That is love itself, that is God, that is what we truly are, and what we truly are we always are, now and for all time and for no time; it is unchanging and always present, ever willing and ready to shine through the shadows of our heads and take us beyond all boundaries and divisions to where we have always been—together in love as love.

REACTING AND RESPONDING

There is a great difference between a passing intellectual interest and a heartfelt and often heart-broken wondering "why" at life, at God, and at ourselves, though in fairness any interest is a good interest. Often in a life crisis the hopes and dreams that are so personal to us and the ones we love, our home, the work we do, and the esteem in which society holds us, which are all important ingredients that go to make up the story we live in, can all be wiped away in a momentary swipe as life makes a mockery out of life. In this kind of dereliction, two things can happen. Pain, they say, is a great healer, but it is also a great destroyer and often kills more people than it heals. Whether or which depends to a large degree on how we are within ourselves when this kind of calamity befalls us. We are all so uniquely individual that it is unwise to generalise the outcome as this is dependent to a large extent on the quality and content of the story in which we are housed, and this is further dependent on our society and all the other aspects of our up-bringing that determines the kind of conditioning we have received. Put in simple terms, it depends on whether we react or respond. We live in a world that is often exclusively reactionary to life situations. We are conditioned to react to what takes place within and programmed to react to outward events. When we look closely at how we react, we find that almost every reaction creates a further reaction and sets in motion a chain of events that mostly makes things worse.

Now if we can respond or at least try to respond rather than react, something entirely different takes place. When I respond to a painful situation, I still feel all the pain, anger, and powerlessness, and that is how it should be. However, because I respond and not react, I don't make it any worse, I don't create more pain or regrets that sentence me to future suffering. By responding I turn into the pain, not away. Responding creates a space that allows for acceptance, and this space is very important. It is the beginning of healing and a surrendering of self-will. A reaction denotes a conditioned ego, while a response says "I don't know" or "I'm not sure."

We seldom take the time to ask if our all too easily constructed idea of what is real is the only reality available to us. If we did, we may become more aware and open-minded. When we live from our heads only, from our cherished beliefs and concepts, then we are almost compelled to react. We are so afraid of being knocked off this standpoint that we become defensive and sometimes aggressive, being happy only if other people agree with us. A reaction is always wrong. A response is entirely different. For instance, in an emergency, if I respond, I will act spontaneously, and a spontaneous action will always be right because there is no ego involved. I am responding from my heart to what is. To act and to react are entirely different forms of action. A reaction comes from my head, from the known and so from the past, and prevents me from living in the now. A response is a present-moment event and stands alone.

If I am always imposing past conditioning on the present, then I am not truly living in the now. We can see that the past and future are from memory. The present also cannot be described as a state because it is ever-changing. Like the flame of a burning candle it appears to be always the same yet it is never the same because it is always new. The same can be said for a river or a stream. Yet it is right here at the almost invisible cutting edge of the constantly fluctuating present that life happens and is always new. To be awake to this truth, to this ghostly encounter, is to live spontaneously. To live a life one day at a time is a tremendous achievement, but to live in the now is the ultimate adventure of human life.

Maybe it is here that the person and the source come face to face, but which face is which? Which part of the candle flame is old and which is new. Is there a space or a gap between the old part of the flame and the new? The answer is no because there can't be an old flame. How could there be, if nothing is ever the same, if nothing stands still? We will often come up against contradictions in the quest for life's deeper meaning. In fact, life itself is a contradiction of gigantic proportions. For instance, if I look up I see a sky, yet there is no sky, it is only light. If I walk west, I am travelling east because my world is turning away from the west. When I look out to sea, there is a straight line that I call the horizon—so straight that builders can take levels from it—yet there is no horizon, it can't be straight, the ocean is not flat but round. The sun does not rise in the east, nor does it set in the west. It may be said that all these statements are relative, but what is relativity? It changes nothing, it is merely a term of reference. We are held on to the side of a large, round object by something called gravity. It flies through endless space at thousands of miles per hour. We know only a little about the other round objects that are closest to us, and that's it. We have no idea of where all this is except in relation to a few other galaxies; in truth, no one knows where we are.

In one of John Moriarty's stories, a drunk man on his journey homeward in the dark keeps asking "Where are we?" as he stumbles forward. He arrives at his own place and asks again "Where are we, John?" After John's full and gentle explanation, he says "Ah, 'tis well I know where we are now, John, 'tis well I know it now, but where the fuck are we?" So we think we know where we are and at the same time we don't know where we are. But these great contradictions need not be the problem, they may well be the solution. They are the mirror that shows me the end of my thinking or maybe that there is no end to my thinking, that there can only be an open-ended, non-descriptive view with an open mind.

HEART BUSINESS ONLY

While we were returning home from a visit to a friend's farm, a question emerged out of the silence. "Is Liam a boy or a girl, Granda?" Somewhat surprised by the suddenness of my grandson's question, I replied, "Liam is a boy, Joseph, and you are a boy." Then the silence fell around us once again, but I inwardly knew that four-year-old Joseph's question and I had some unfinished business.

This was not the first time Joseph had taken me into a world of virgin innocence, a place where, sadly, adulthood seldom lingers. In attempting to fully understand Joseph's question, I knew my finest thinking was going to let me down. His was a pathless land of total perception, where intuitive intelligence was the only currency in circulation. At first glance this would appear to be a question about gender; was he attempting to understand why his friend Liam was a boy and not a girl, and was he, by looking outside of himself to Liam, really looking inward at himself with the same question? Or perhaps his question holds a more primal significance, one that we as adults have long forgotten. Supposing he is asking "Why do I have to be a boy or a girl? I am happy to remain as I am, just being, without being anything in particular."

This is not a question from the point of view of being a body. This is a question from pure, undivided, undifferentiated awareness, where the controlling power of thought as yet holds no sway. Here all business is heart business only; head business—that is, thought and thinking—takes its place amongst all other events on the periphery of importance.

"Man divides in thought what is undivided in nature," Alan Watts wrote. "The fall, as it is known in old world language, never was about sex. It concerns the gradual movement into self-consciousness that up until then was not conscious of itself at all. It was collective . . . universal, there was nothing personal about it, there still isn't, we only feel there is, and that's the falling into individuality, into ego; it is the feeling of being a me, which formally was a feeling of simply being."

Joseph the four-year-old lives in and from the very heart of totality, from his whole being, which we call the heart or soul. Now slowly but surely the feeling of living in his head is gradually coming over him. The movie camera of life is zooming in on individuality rather than the big picture of life and living complete. Consciousness, not conscious of itself is being traded in for a smaller model of *self*-consciousness. This is a downsizing through thought. What Joseph was really asking is "why", and to do so he has to use whatever language is available to him through thought. When you consider that thought is words without sound, we are getting to the heart of the whole business, because thought by its very nature is a limiting experience. The more thinking that takes place, the smaller life becomes. Gradually it gets reduced to the round ball that sits at the top of our bodies. Life as we then see it is an embodied experience. I am now in here and the environment is out there.

They say that long-term prisoners become institutionalised because they find it impossible to imagine living any other kind of life. Sadly we all become institutionalised, long-term prisoners of self-consciousness. Through the many shades of thought we feel limited to being male or female, young or old, living or dying; what we then take ourselves to be depends entirely on the kind of body we have staked our lives on.

When the body is in full working order we say we are alive, when it breaks down and the all important heart stops working, others say we are dead, but are we? Aren't we forgetting that all this identification with individuality, with being a body, a person, started and developed through thinking. Prior to this there was a body, and the life-giving consciousness, but not yet self-consciousness. Consciousness dose not arrive with the body, it exists always, and remains blissfully unaffected by creation or destruction of any kind.

"Understand that it is not the individual which has consciousness. It is the consciousness which assumes innumerable forms"—Nisargadatta Maharaj.

We think our way into living in a body, into living a life so long as the body lives, and in so doing we think ourselves to death also. We hope for a life after death, but no one gives any attention to life before birth. Our prison time is served in institutionalised thinking. We gradually accept it for better or worse, as being the way life is. We become unable to imagine otherwise—until one day suddenly an unexpected voice comes from our homeland of living innocence with a question that, no matter how it is answered, still remains a question unanswered. In Joseph's homeland and ours its nature remains unspoken and unworded. That is why, despite all the comings and goings, there are no chains that bind, nor locks that hold fast the ever-open gates of our eternally ever-present life in Paradise, not lost, nor left.

OUR SLEEP OF EARTH

To say that there is no such thing as a person is a very strong statement indeed. Here we are speaking absolutely and not relatively. Let us return to the state of the infant in its mother's womb: even when it was just a little speck of matter without shape or form, it was aware, because this awareness is always present. It is not in need of anything to support it, neither a body nor a brain, nor self-consciousness; it is prior to everything and nothing, it is the background of all that is, it is life eternal, it needs neither time nor space. Nothing can exist without this awareness. We call it spirit or god or the father or godhead or soul or life and thousands of other names. This awareness never changes and is unaffected by anything whatsoever; everything exists in and because of it. There is nothing that is outside of it, neither consciousness nor universes nor all the worlds ever imagined or known; it is what links you to me. In fact, this awareness is what we are, not separate bits of awareness, just awareness.

Now let's deal with how the feeling or idea of being a separate individual comes about because this is the heart of the whole matter. This is so important, yet so simple. We return again to the tiny, shapeless particle of matter in the womb. When

> *What will you do now with the gift of your left life?*
> CAROL ANN DUFFY

nine months later it emerges as an infant, having developed without any outside help, it knows that it exists and is aware, not aware of being this or that, just aware. So the little infant is in a state of grace and completeness and wholeness or holiness. There is no sense of being an individual, of having been born, of having any particular shape; there is as yet no ego.

Have you ever noticed how good it feels to hold and cuddle a baby or just lay beside them when they are sleeping? They radiate a peace and serenity that puts us in touch with something we seem to have lost or find only now and then, a presence that is also to be felt in the company of certain gentle, egoless people. The infant remains in paradise until, for no apparent reason, thinking and memory combine to bring the "me" feeling, and the fall from paradise begins. The silken threads of joyful peace are being stretched and the light of common day begins to break through. The infant starts to identify with the body, which up to now it was gloriously oblivious to. The sense of separation increases and so the seeds of being an individual are sown. With the arrival of thought also comes memory, and this acts to strengthen the idea of being a person. With memory comes the idea of a thinker who can think thoughts and so the whole illusion of a person continues to deepen and take hold. With memory, of course, also comes the concept of time. Memory brings us a past, even though we can only at any given time have a present momentary thought of a past event; we cannot at any time have an old memory, or old thought, only a present thought. We are, nonetheless, slipping further away from our true state of oneness and wholeness. This, of course, is all taking place at a mental level only. It is a sense or a feeling. This bundle of thoughts and feelings we call a person is simply a case of mistaken identity. A body was born and exists with all its genetically inherited characteristics, but consciousness or awareness has always been present, even before the arrival of the body. It is only with the arrival of thought, or rather the identification of consciousness with thought, that the idea of a separate person comes into being. We say the person was born; what was born was an idea and a feeling which we call ego—admittedly a bewitching feeling, but a feeling nonetheless. With the feeling "this is me", or "I am this", comes the concept of space, which intensifies the feeling of separation. If this is me, then that is not me—a space or distance has now appeared between me and the not me, which did not previously exist and which in truth does not exist; it just appears to with the thought "this is me."

The concept of time is completed when we recall the already experienced, superimposing it on the now as something that may or may not happen, and in so doing imagine into action what we call the future, which is out ahead somewhere, and we are caught up in a kind of time philosophy. The future, we feel, will always be better than the present or the past. We often use this as a means of escaping the harshness of the present, or sometimes as a way of escaping from our fear of death and from our vulnerability; we feel safer with a future out ahead. The ego, of course, does not really have any solid ground of its own. It is just a sense or feeling, looking to the past or the known for support and to the future for safety. Like the pendulum of a clock, it swings from past to future and future to past, never coming to rest in the present. We are always escaping from the now, because in the now there is no time. The ego will violently resist the idea of no future—thus the fear of dying and letting go. There is no such thing as time in absolute truth. What we call time is relative to memory, ego, and thought. A body is born and goes through its span of life, and all its actions have universal causes; consciousness is the creating force of all that lives, including the body and all its actions, the ability to feel, think, and work through all the senses. There is no room for a person in all this or no need. It is only when we see behind this great and wonderful illusion or trick of the mind that we can have real love and compassion for the persons we think we are. We learn to remain as the witness to all the events of life with a detached compassion. We stop judging ourselves and others, we stop fighting life and ourselves, we begin to feel and glimpse the timeless now—and, as we have seen above, it is always now; there never was any other time. Now is the only fact; the rest is created by thought, a thought being only a movement in consciousness. When consciousness is at rest, like in a dreamless sleep, the world, the person, and the body disappear; only awareness remains, pure awareness, the light of life and love. How far we have strayed from our home; ejected by a projection, by a reflection, we wander, seeking everywhere for fulfilment, for happiness, finding it here and there and now and again. We dream we are awake and we dream we are asleep and we dream that we are dreaming but everything seems so real, it just can't be only a dream. But is it only a dream—just like when I am asleep at night I dream I am a great football player, playing for my country, the fans all going wild with delight. Then somebody in the crowd calls me over and tells me I am dreaming and that I am really lying in my bed asleep and I say "But this is real, I am real, all the people at the match are real, the pitch and other players are real. Look at them, you must be crazy to tell me that I am dreaming. I love all this, I want it to last forever. I don't want to die, I don't want to wake up."

But wait a minute . . . maybe to die is to wake up.

"Out of the sleep of earth, with visions rife,
I woke one clear morning full of light
and I said to God whose face made all things bright
that was an awful dream I had last night"—Anon.

The truth is that we cannot know what we truly are; we can only know what we are not. At this level we can only be the truth, because what we truly are is purely subjective. There is nothing objective whatsoever. There is no knower to know anything and nothing to be known. There is only knowing.

There is nothing in any of this asking you to believe what you have read. This is not about belief, even as second-hand information; its limited benefit is as a pointer, a wake-up call and a signpost to the truth that you are. There is nothing to be given and nothing that can be taken away. There is nothing to do and no-one to do it. Just be. To realise what we are does not require an exhaustive study of great books nor great wisdom. It can happen right now, this instant. It is not just for a few, it is for all.

WHO ARE YOU?

Who are you? Have you ever wondered why it's so hard being you, just you? When you think of yourself, is it not mostly in relation to people, entities, or things that you feel best express who you are? Yet regardless of how close the relationship between you and they may be, they are not you. To get a deeper understanding of how difficult it is being just you, we must return back to where "being you" first ran into difficulties. Firstly we will look at some of the outside influences that appear to forever marry you off to what is other than your essential self.

The first to enter the equation, even before you have a chance to see Planet Earth for yourself, are two people called parents who until sometime previously were total strangers and who are now proclaiming that you are their baby. When you finally arrive to see things for yourself yet even more strangers come along, who in turn inform you that they are your brothers, your sisters, your grandparents, your uncles and aunts, your cousins, and so on. The doctor says you are his patient, the priest says you are his parishioner, the teacher says you are her pupil; the country in which you were born says you are its citizen and even has a piece of paper to prove it. Next, you will be someone's boyfriend or girlfriend, and after that maybe you will be someone's husband or wife or partner; then maybe you will be someone's father or mother. You will probably be someone's employee or employer, while the bank manager says you are his customer. Eventually the undertaker gets in on the act, and says you are his corpse, at which point the priest might say "No, no, you belong to God, and it is to him you now return."

What all this amounts to is that whoever you are, you haven't had much chance to be you. So who are you? You are probably thinking that the only way to find the answer is to get away from all these people to some strange land where your face remains private property and where no one calls your name. Perhaps then you will find yourself. Except that you won't. Why? For one thing, you carry your DNA right along with you, a blueprint from your parents and all the parents before them, who live on to one degree or another in your personality and your behaviour. This genetic programming is your inheritance from both the living and the dead, and, whether you like it or not, it gathers itself together to constitute the greater part of that body-mind apparatus you refer to as you.

Then there's the whole business of your conditioning, the kind of environment in which you were raised as a child, the education you received, the social climate, whether your background was privileged or underprivileged, and so on. If you are now thinking this is all too much, I am afraid there's more. Just listen to Friederich Nietzsche: "I have discovered for myself that the old human and animal life, indeed the entire prehistory and past of all sentient being, works on, loves on, hates on, thinks on in me." It now appears your family tree is becoming more of a jungle than a tree, and while jungles can provide shelter and substance for both the individual and the tribe, they are also easy to become lost in and difficult to get out of. As a philosopher, Nietzsche inquired into this whole business very deeply and encountered first hand for himself the difficulties that lay therein: "The individual has always had to struggle to keep from being overwhelmed by the tribe; if you try it you will be lonely often, but no price is too high to pay for the privilege of owning yourself."

Being overwhelmed is something human beings have become accustomed to, so much so that we don't call it overwhelming any more, we call it stress; some even suggest that a little of it is good for us, and while that may well be so, the danger is that we become lost in forgetfulness to the possibility of there being any other way to live. Another hurdle along the road to owning yourself is thrown up by the fact that human beings are highly imitative creatures. This in some ways has probably contributed favourably to our survival as a species, and while this gift for imitation holds as true today as in any previous time, we rather strangely prefer to think of ourselves as essentially independent creatures, as being more individual than tribal. But for all that we are a people who in the main are easily led. Whether through religion, politics or through some self-destructive urge for personal prestige, or the unnecessary prostituting of our souls to acquire other people's money with a fervour once reserved for the appeasing of similar false gods, is it not obvious something is leading us to overreact and overreach? What all these behavioural tendencies have in common is they betray a deep insecurity at the very heart of our humanity, even among those who appear to have full and plenty. Our lessons, it seems, seldom come easy; our tendency to first take most things to an extreme before finally returning to some kind of equilibrium means we are continually returning to close the stable door after our horses have bolted for the greener pastures of hope over experience.

Speaking of horses, and before you saddle and ride off into the sunset, hoping to find yourself, consider that no matter how fast or how far or what direction you ride in, you will be taking the one you wish to find right along with you. In fact all outward searching for your true self is doomed to lead you in ever-increasing circles away from that which you wish to be united with because, no matter what circumstances you find yourself in, and regardless of what duties and demands imprison your attention and freedom, your true inner you is waiting always to reveal itself unconditionally. Except discovering it requires you get off your horse, hang the bridle of your important self upon the wall, smoke your pipe of rest . . . and wait.

ETERNITY IS NOW

When I am aware of a thought like "I see a mountain", I then have the feeling that I am thinking the thought "I see a mountain", but this is itself just another thought. It gives the feeling that there is some "one" who is a separate and independent entity who has had a thought, but the reality is it is just another thought. No matter how hard you try you will never find the thinker of the thoughts because there isn't one. There's only thinking and no separate thinker. The same, of course, can be said for seeing, hearing, and smelling. You can never see the seer, hear the hearer, or smell the smeller of the smell. There is only the sensation of seeing, hearing, and smelling.

You are a king that has settled for being a beggar. You have accepted mistakenly that you were born with this body you call you and you live in the terror of a certain death that has you constantly demanding a future, and this prevents you from living in the now. Memory convinces you that you have a past, but any memory is still just a present thought.

121

You can never have an old or past thought, you can only have a present thought of the already experienced. Everything happens in the timeless, present moment. Eternity is "now". Eternal life is "now". You live now. You have always lived and will always live now regardless of what happens to the physical body, because you, as awareness, were present before the body was conceived and born. You are present during the life span of the body and you will remain present after the death of the body. You have always been aware and conscious. You are aware and conscious right now. This conscious awareness is not dependent on anything—not a body, nor any god or godlike presence that is imagined as being separate from the awareness you are. There is no separation of any kind whatsoever, absolutely none. There never has been. You are God, you are the life and the light, the truth and the presence. You are the one and only. It is you who look out from behind my eyes and I who look out from behind your eyes because we are the one awareness, one god and one presence. Let the events of worldly life come and go, let birth and death come and go because neither affliction nor crucifixion can affect what we are as awareness.

Understanding is the great liberator. To understand something at profound level, our intuitive intelligence needs to emerge out of the shadows where it has been consigned in

122

favour of our thinking ability, our new god. Almost all the great insights that have profoundly changed human life have come about as a spontaneous, intuitive knowing. There would, of course, have been much searching and the heartfelt desire to know, but the final answer comes in a flash. This is true both of the mystic and the scientist. These intuitive insights rarely if ever come while we are thinking. Usually they suddenly strike us while we are doing something utterly unrelated to the problem we are trying to solve. Often when reading or listening to a discussion on some subject we may experience difficulty and think "all this is beyond me".

> *Once educated, a mind is no longer as transformatively available to alternative intuition as it originally was*
> JOHN MORIARTY

This happens simply because we are unable to think of the answer right away. If I don't understand it right now, then it is beyond me. In these wonderful times, information and answers are generally available in an instant in a few clicks. We also expect our minds to react in a similar manner; the answer must be worked out and understood right now. This is understandable for most of life in today's world, but there are other aspects of our lives that do not dance to this instant tune, and it is here that we do a great injustice to ourselves and life. We can run a narrow road through life, if that is what we think is best, ignoring the mountains, the valleys, the oceans, and all the great questions they ask of us, questions that sometimes cause an uneasy stirring in our hearts and heads. However, if we keep our heads down and mind our narrow road we will be okay, or so we think. To live life in this way might be the only way possible for some less able for the open road, and that's fair enough. However, a life lived in a partial way is not really living at all. There is an uneasiness inherent in the human condition that cannot be pushed aside or always ignored. It may go unrecognised but it is there nonetheless, and like the everyday workings of nature, or what we call nature, it demands an answer even though we might not always have heard the question. There is something within us and something without that seems to have us constantly reaching outwards. There are questions inherent in all of life that we ignore or cast aside at our peril. To live a life on the open road demands an openness of mind we are seldom able or willing to subscribe to. This mostly comes about because of our refusal to accept our personal powerlessness. That little person who lives in our head, whom we take to be "me", fights off on all sides any suggestion of powerlessness or any thought of not being in charge, now and for all time. How small and narrow this standpoint seems for those who have hit the open road and climbed to where the view is much different. Not long after the death of his four-year-old son, Thomas Henry Huxley wrote: "Science seems to me to teach in the highest and strongest manner the great truth which is embodied in the Christian conception of entire surrender to the will of God. Sit down before the fact as a little child, be prepared to give up every preconceived notion, follow humbly wherever and to whatever abyss nature leads, or you shall learn nothing."

Our smallness is sometimes exploded unceremoniously before our very eyes, our lessons learned often coming about as a result of a great personal tragedy or a crisis not of our own making. Crises often have the effect of shocking us into the realisation of how powerless we actually are as individuals. In Huxley's case, the devastating death of his little boy brings about a humility of looking we can all learn from, which is all too often missing from our worldly human condition. The term "open-mindedness" is bandied about with an arrogance that holds little of the humility demonstrated here by Huxley. How painful and often aggravating it is to listen to supposedly intellectual arguments about whether or not there is a God. It can only be placed on the archaic level of argument as to whether the world was round or flat, or whether the earth circled the sun or vice versa. In any searching, scientific or otherwise, if I ask the wrong question I will inevitably receive the wrong answer or no answer at all. We can talk all we wish of gods and the Big Bang, exploding and imploding universes and still have only opinions, theories, and concepts to assault one another with. Now all this may be very well intentioned. The problem, of course, is that with this kind of looking we are looking outward and we fail to ask the all important question—"Who is doing the looking?" Until this question is addressed, all we can have is second-hand knowledge and outside information. Our ego, that small "I" within my head that we generally take to be all that we are, by its very nature resists any attempts at introspection, unless for one reason or another we have been gifted with a natural but uncommon humility. Thus comes the need for most of us to be rendered in some way helpless by a crisis of life before we become like a child again, innocent before the fact that can't be denied, no matter how we try or how hard we wish it isn't so. To be brought like a child before the fact, we usually need to feel profoundly powerless. Of course, people differ, egos vary, and one man's tragedy might only be another man's problem. There is no strict rule by which all might be measured.

Another problem arises here, which has been well documented through the ages by mystics and others who have travelled the inward road. These hardy souls would universally agree that the ego, though sometimes greatly reduced, will always use every possible avenue to reassert itself. Thus arises the need for a continual voluntary surrender to the will of God, the spirit of the universe, or whatever name we choose to give a power greater than ourselves. This is a surrendering of our cherished so-called free will and the idea that as independent separate individuals we can do as we like. This voluntary surrender to the greater good, the greater order, can bring about much inner conflict at first, unless a deeper understanding of the nature of the ego is attained. There is a hugely important difference between taking on the ego in a head-to-head fight and in understanding the nature of the ego and how it comes about in the first place. In most, if not all, areas of life, understanding reduces conflict because understanding brings humility, and humility is what love comes wrapped up in. To take up violence against the ego, the body, or any other aspect of what we are is a crime against all that we are spiritually. Understanding, born of inquiry and the need to know, is what sets us truly and unconditionally free. In this wonderful age of information, surely it is not too much to ask that we inquire out of love into our true identity and, on discovering the unearthly magnitude of our true greatness, we become the best human beings we can possibly be.

A THIRST UNQUENCHED

There has always been a lost wondering in the human mind, something that just does not feel right, a kind of yearning, a longing for some kind of completeness. We are not always aware of this need, but it is always there in the background, emerging in many guises. It is sometimes felt as a kind of divine dissatisfaction. It is the call of the wild, the untamed, and appears to come from somewhere beyond. It is in answer to this call that the mystics of all ages have been compelled to travel beyond the human mind, beyond the safety and restrictions of words, symbols, and thinking.

A child separated from its mother on a busy street cries in pain—a soul pain. The child may be comforted by kind and loving strangers but the pain remains. Soul pain is loss pain—something is missing. The sense of separation creates a bottomless pit, and even though everything that life can give is placed into the pit, it still remains empty. When the child is reunited with its mother, it once again feels safe and in every way complete. In the warmth of unity, soul pain ceases. Humankind too has soul pain and it is in attempting to diagnose the cause of this pain that most of our spiritual and religious problems occur. When any teaching, belief system or philosophy fails to embrace the underlying unity of all things and the divine ground, there occurs a problem of such magnitude that, from this initial blunder, springs a man-made vacuum that condemns its exponents and others to half truths and half answers. Only when the child discovered it was not really lost at all, and that it only appeared to be lost, was it happy and complete. Only when human beings realise that they too only appear to be separate

> *There should be no premature closing of our account with reality*
>
> WILLIAM JAMES

from God, or the divine ground, is that inner feeling of loss and separation dissolved into love.

The responsibility of all spiritual teachers is to point out the absence of any separation whatsoever and therefore rule out the possibility of birth, life, or death having any effect, good, bad, or indifferent, on what we truly are. Any philosophy or teaching that deviates from this fundamental truth fails in every sense in its responsibility to those it professes to help. When any fragmented view of the nature of life is embraced, trouble always follows automatically. To say that something imperfect can come from the all-perfect, all-embracing is a contradiction. The all-embracing means that all is within and all is one—that nothing is outside, so where the divine ground is concerned there can be nothing other than itself, nothing is secondary and nothing in the manifested world or any other world can be imperfect or apart from the divine ground or the self. I am that and so are you. To see the great tragedy and stupendous foolishness of any religious teaching or philosophy that is obsessed and addicted to human individuality and separateness, we need only take a brief glimpse at the words of the various mystics who were speaking from experience and attempting, in so far as they were able, to transfer their realisation into the written word.

William Law: "Heaven is as near to our souls as this world is to our bodies . . . We are all of us by birth the offspring of God, more nearly related to him than we are to one another for in Him we live and move and have our being."

Pierre Teilhard de Chardin: "I live in the heart of a single element, the centre and detail of all personal love and cosmic power."

Sri Ramana Maharshi: "You are the self, nothing but the self, anything else is just imagination, so be the self here and now, carry on with your essential activities, but free yourself from association with the doer of them. Self is the witness—you are that."

From century to century, the words of the mystics may change—different words for different times—but what never changes is the essence of what the words attempt to convey. The period the mystics emerge from is unimportant, as is where they came from or what religion or philosophy they held or has since been attributed to them. Many of the great seers and mystics, in fact, would not have had any particular religiously structured thought, but they would have been adopted or claimed by different religions. In truth, however, most religions seem to take little or no interest in the teachings of these path-finders. Instead they are content to preach an unenlightened misinterpretation and seem obsessed with sex, with sinful bodies, and something called moral behaviour. This has failed. There has been no worthwhile transformation in the heart of man. All this in an age of admirable progress in most other aspects, but within the heart of humankind little or no change has taken place. Now even a passing interest in the teachings of the mystics, past and present, should present us with a glimpse of our own true greatness as collective consciousness. It is we who put on the greatest show on earth: we script, produce, direct, and star in our ever-changing spiritual production—the longest running show in town, which seldom gets the awards it deserved. Probably the saddest omission of all is that we rarely give ourselves the credits we are entitled to. However, once we take a step in the right direction there is a chance of the rhythm of our inner world and the rhythm of the universe coming together to reveal our divine unity which, speaking absolutely, is all inclusive because in it all our apparent differences and separations and all our wrongs and rights remain divine and at peace within the brightness of home, something that prompted Thomas à Kempis to declare: "If thy heart were right, then every creature would be a mirror of life and a Book of Holy Doctrine."

GREAT AND SMALL

Over the past one hundred years, the thinking mind of Western man has brought about a huge change for the better in our daily standard of living. The industrial revolution and the quantum leap from science fiction to science fact leaves us standing in admiration at the ingenious mind of modern man. We reap the benefits of scientific thinking in our everyday lives from the comfort of our own homes to our places of work where thinking man has made life the easiest it has ever been. It is understandable therefore why it is difficult for most people to accept the idea that deep within the deepest recesses of their being there lies an even greater self that transcends body, mind, space, and time. That there exists some power or intelligence that transcends our human mind and the power of thought is not at all easy for an educated person to accept. Life today is so fulfilling for most of us in Western society that there scarcely seems to be any need to reach out for something greater than our human selves. For far too long the vulnerable human psyche was a slave to the thinking of others who often claimed and exercised a spiritual right they did not have. The ignorance of the vulnerable served as the planting ground where the ignorant educated fulfilled their hunger for power and their personal need for superiority at the expense others. The unhealthy, often tragic consequences of this scenario, which was damaging to all concerned, was a church or a power structure that expected the people to serve it. Today if people are part of a church or religious structure, they expect and demand to be served and not to serve. This would seem to be a much safer and spiritually rewarding arrangement for all involved. Individuals now possess and enjoy the ability to do their own thinking, and this has brought about a huge shift, not alone in what is taught, but more importantly in what is being accepted. The impoverished and sometimes non-existent mystical spirituality that past generations were forced to endure has played a major role in some of the sadder aspects of society today. The grave ills of most societies cannot be explained entirely by pointing the finger at sexual revolutions, so-called declining morals, or any of the other convenient activities where blame can be easily laid. When the majesty of the human body has been constantly demeaned and sexuality is seen only as an activity for human procreation, a great psychic vacuum is created and this sets in motion within the human mind the poverty of suppression, inner guilt, denial, and rejection. These are some of the building blocks of unhealthy mental states, which always have detrimental consequences for the individual and society alike. Anything within me that I suppress or deny will eventually come back to haunt and/or attack me in another form. Any denial of what may be considered as dark in me will usually result in me unconsciously projecting what I dislike in myself on to others. I will then hate the other person for their faults, which in reality are only my own unconscious guilt projections of all I dislike in myself. I then look out at a hostile world that threatens to attack me at every opportunity and so I am now out of harmony with myself and my environment. And if this sad state of affairs is coupled with an almost non-existent knowledge of my own spiritual nature, then trouble surely follows, not just for me but also for my everyday living world.

Any narrow, impoverished view of myself, mentally or spiritually, affects not just me in the personal sense, but also the society of which I am a part. What I am inside my head has a direct relationship to what is outside and beyond my head. The same, of course, can be said for society; it also has a direct influence for better or worse on the individual. As individuals we all affect one another, even those we have never even met. We can be forgiven for thinking that mind is individual and private only, and that what happens in my mind concerns me alone. This, I feel, is the generally accepted view, that somehow we are isolated and independent units, cut off and separated mentally from one another and physically by the boundaries of our skin. On the surface this seems a reasonable enough view of how we are. However, those who have carried the investigation a little deeper have discovered a mind that is not the property of any individual, great or small. It has been aptly termed the collective unconscious by Carl Jung—also the universal mind, mind at large, and many other names by the various mystics and seers down through the ages. Because we are self-conscious and we think of ourselves as individuals only, we restrict ourselves to the particular and consider the collective to be other than ourselves. We are continuously making all things great into all things small. We consistently, and without knowing it, create our own hell and then try to seek

135

every possible means of escape. Maybe it is because we have lived for so long in the absence of any worthwhile spiritual education directing our hearts towards the transcendental and our home that we have forgotten our eternal greatness and have settled for less than we are entitled to. To cling to this shadowy body for safety and security is to always find myself standing on thin ice. It holds me up but it doesn't guarantee me the feeling of contentment and restfulness I desperately need. Taking this body to be all that I am and all that I can be, I am like the person who has lived all his life in complete darkness and who, on emerging into the sunlight, takes his shadow to be who he is. The reflection of the sun on the dew drop is bewitching indeed, but it is not the sun, it is only the sunlight. Likewise, our self consciousness or the "me" feeling is not consciousness itself, but one of the special effects of consciousness—awareness. Just as the sun itself is not affected in any way by the effects and actions of its light, what I truly am (awareness) is not in any way affected by all that I give life and existence to. This body, this person, this world, and all other worlds are dependent on what I am for their existence, but I am not dependent upon them for my existence. This is the big picture, and the rest are special effects and nothing else. Now can we see how ridiculous and sad it is to live life as an effect; it is little wonder that we find ourselves in the sad state of affairs where our humanity groans under its own weight and where no fundamental change has taken place within the heart of humankind despite the passing of time and the many wonderful changes that have taken place for the better.

The reason that no fundamental shift has come about in human consciousness is precisely because we remain obsessed with our earthly bodies as individuals. Also most organised religions and belief systems are similarly obsessed with the human body and the human mind or thinking process. The emphasis has been misplaced. We have glorified the shadow and, in doing so, turned our back on the substance. We rarely, if ever, turn our face to the light, preferring in our educated ignorance to fumble onwards into our false god of time, stopping now and again to give praise to or seek wise counsel from our false god away in some heavenly sky. Meanwhile, back in the shadows, we treat one another with the same abominable contempt and murderous righteousness as did our distant predecessors, with perhaps one important difference—our forefathers did not have the benefit of the information and learning that we now enjoy. They can be excused; we cannot. The great poverty of our society, which has no regard for spirituality, lies everywhere to be seen. We can change the surface ills of our time all we please, we can legislate, officiate, and departmentalise as much as we like, yet at a deep and substantial level no change has come about in the heart of the individual.

There has always been a natural yearning in the heart of the human spirit. This longing or restlessness could be described more as a need. While this need for fulfilment is often mistakenly understood to be a poverty and a need of something to be made whole, the very opposite is in fact the case, for within the divine ground, our true home, there is no need or wanting whatsoever. The expression of the spirit takes place simply because it is within its nature to do so. Far from needing something to be whole or complete, the spirit awareness is magnificently expressing its fullness. Now when I as a human being or ego centre become addicted to the power of the thinking mind and the misplaced total identification with the human form, it is the "me" who suffers and is in need, never the spirit or divine ground of the "I" that foreverI am.

OUR FORMER GLORY

D o not worry about how you spend your life because it is life that lives you. There is no such thing as free will. We as persons are mostly either responding or reacting to thoughts and other stimuli that come through the senses, giving the impression that there is a person inside the body directing, choosing, and taking responsibility for all acts and actions. Nothing could be further from the truth. The fact is that we become prisoners of an ego that does not exist. Is this not the final insult—am I just nothing, a nothing? Well, not really. Because everything that has ever been has been because you are. Everything that is, is because you are. Everything that will ever be can only be because you are. You are the life in every life that has ever lived; every pair of eyes that has ever looked out at the world for all time, you have looked through them; every flower that has danced in the wind, you have given it life—you are also the wind, the rain, and the sunshine. There is nothing that you are not, all exists within you as consciousness and nothing is outside . . . all is one and one is all. You and I have always been in love because we are love. We are the dust that returns to dust, the ashes that return to ashes, the life that returns to the life that in truth it never left. Just as the sun did not move to appear in the dew drop, but was just reflected, we too are reflected in the light of life. There is no reason for all this, it just is. Why should there be a reason? There is neither a beginning nor an ending, like the grass that grows because its nature is to do so. There is no why, only why not. So if to die is to wake up, was that what prompted Wordsworth to proclaim "our birth is but a sleep and a forgetting"? But we don't completely forget our former glory. There is something we can't quite remember, and there is something we can't quite forget. The truth is we seek it all the time. Almost all of our actions in life are motivated by a search for happiness, a moment of wholeness, a self-forgetting into freedom where there is no want, no brokenness, no need, and the dualistic mind is still, the pendulum has come to rest in the wholeness and completeness of the eternal now. In this special timeless present what has happened is not that we have acquired something new, rather we have glimpsed and been gifted something older than old, something that is with us all the time but is somehow shaded from our view by a mist or a fog that is there and yet not there. When the pendulum of life starts to swing again and consciousness becomes self-conscious, there is identification with thoughts, with name and form, and the fog again settles and obscures our true nature, pure awareness.

140

Our happiest moments are those self-forgetting moments when we are not self-conscious yet conscious. At night we prepare a place to sleep that is usually dark and quiet, so as to deny our senses any stimulation. We want the theatre in our heads to stop, even preferring if possible not to have dreams. On waking and realising that we had a wonderful dreamless sleep, we feel refreshed and peaceful. So what has happened to bring about this much sought-after feeling? We simply have died to self. The person, the thinking process, the whole process of objectifying, of remembering and projecting has ceased, and only awareness, not self-awareness, is present. But awareness has not just appeared, awareness is always present. The body sleeps soundly but awareness

Of something felt like something here, of something done I know not where, such as no language may declare

ALFRED LORD TENNYSON

never sleeps or changes in any way whatsoever, it is always present. Only when consciousness stirs a little do we dream and a whole dream world is created. When the body comes to life, another world appears and the waking process starts again.

Any time we are not self-conscious is our most peaceful time. We fear death, we fear the unknown, we fear letting go of our feelings, of not being in control. When we think of these things, we feel uncomfortable and we usually push these thoughts away. We suppress our fear and our discomfort, but anything I suppress will always come back to visit me in some other way.

And yet despite all my fears of death, when I sleep I die to everything. I have no guarantee whatsoever that I will wake up. I die to my family, responsibilities, my future, and to all I hold dear, yet I don't give it a second thought, and gladly surrender to the night. Of course, the physical body obviously needs rest, but there is much more to sleep than just that. If I don't sleep for some reason or other, I feel dull and irritable, my mind has not been rested, or maybe it is I who have not been rested from my mind. Even in the waking state there are times when I wish I could escape the mental frequency I seem to be tuned into. There is no "on" and "off" button, except perhaps some kind of mental acrobatics by way of distraction, like taking a mood altering substance of some kind, or engaging in some physical activity, so sleep is the great escape, and a very necessary one.

But who is it that has to escape? When we look dispassionately at the mind, as if somehow from outside, a division seems to appear, a witness emerges, and we start to get a

142

glimpse of the true position. That which fears death is simply the ego or thinking process, which often appears to have a mind of its own. It is thought that prevents us from seeing and knowing our essential unity, our true homeland. When the mind forgets itself, consciousness shines forth in all its splendour, like the sun when the clouds have passed by. Our bodies live out their time and dance to nature's tune. The body doesn't say "I fear death, I don't want to die." The awareness, consciousness or spirit does not fear death, it doesn't even know birth or death. Only the person I think I am, this bundle of thoughts, memories, and projections, fears death. The shadow feels vulnerable, the substance fears nothing. Once this is seen, we can live in peace, because peace is what we are. The person I am can only be truly loved by me when there is an understanding of what constitutes me as a person. Compassion and acceptance spring from understanding. Only then is fear embraced and not suppressed or ignored, only then am I able to live vulnerably, which is to live with the facts—and to live with the truth is to truly live. To be at peace with myself is to be at peace with others and all that is other than me. To see the great beauty in all created things, I first have to see the stupendous beauty in myself.

LOVE CHILD

When we take ourselves to be less than we are, we will always feel less: we create a problem where there is no problem, a division where there formerly was none, and from both sides of this divide we do battle within ourselves and seldom call a truce or know the kind of peace and safety that is our birthright.

If only once in a while I could put off all my knowing and conclusions, if I could once again stand in that childlike innocence and be entertained by the works of God in all their pre-educated splendour, I might enter the kingdom of heaven. Of course, the pre-educated, unconditioned child doesn't have to enter heaven; they never left. Someone once said "How strange it is that a child can know the secrets that the books of the learned never unfold."

Let us love the child in ourselves, let us love the love that animates our earthly splendour. It may be the only thing worth living for, or indeed the only thing worth dying for. To die to our name and form is the only death that is necessary . . . an idea is born and an idea dies, nothing happens. We live in a world, as Shakespeare said, "of sound and fury that signifies nothing." Like the morning mist it is there, yet not there. It can be touched but not held, lived only in the ever-present now. The only significance that life has is in the present moment; it can only be lived in the now, and at no other time. I have often wondered about this when I am part of a crowd of thirty to forty thousand people at a football match and nothing else in life really matters at that time because of the drama and excitement—yet if I come back to the stadium later that evening there is nothing, just a field. What has happened, where has it all gone? I could see it and feel it; now it is as though it never happened. I can never again touch that wonderful time. I can't turn back the clock. I can't even stop the clock. Perhaps to live a life in time is to never have our feet on solid ground. It is no wonder we feel afraid and threatened.

When we mourn someone who has died, part of that mourning has to do with coming face to face with our own mortality. We feel uncomfortable because we see our projections of a future, secure life for what they are—just thoughts, hopes, and dreams. There is no place to lay our heads because we can't stop, we can't get off, life won't let us. When we live out of our heads only, we live in time, and to live in time is to inhabit a lonely, ever-changing landscape. If, however, we can touch or be touched by something that is timeless, only then does the landscape start to change and take on a new, welcoming presence.

For instance, when we gaze across the ocean, all we can see is a never-ending movement as the waves continually tumble towards the shore and the water heaves between trough and crest. If, however, we were to travel below the surface, the further down we went the calmer and stiller it would be. So the constant movement and change is not all there is; it just appears that way on the surface. Often we think that what we see, experience, and know is all there is. We stand on the shores of life and say "This is it: birth, life, and death." But this is a narrow view of life; if it is not accessible to the senses and to the mind, we feel it is not real and we can't know for sure, so we cling to the little we do know and we live in our heads, hoping and praying they won't let us down. We fight and kill one another for what is in our heads, for what we think. We worship God with one idea and kill all around us with another. We live and die in our heads without ever having really lived at all. We continue to admire the wrapping on the present without ever thinking of opening it up to see what is inside. We are satisfied, it seems, with just the wrapping, or are we?

ME THINKING

I t is not fair to say absolutely that life and the world is an illusion, a dream. It is not, because life and all the contents of life have their own relative reality. What is unreal and illusory, however, is the way we perceive it to be. Not only that, but we are also confused about what is doing the creating and the perceiving.

Adding further to our dilemma is the belief that by changing the person I take myself to be, I will grow spiritually. But what is the point of cleaning the face of the multi-headed monster, the ego? It seems like a good idea at the time, and the monster likes it very much and will gladly accommodate you. But no matter how hard you work, there will always be a new face to clean.

You may also trawl about in what you consider to be your unconscious or rummage around in the already known, which you call the past, but to little or no avail as far as knowing the self, the absolute, is concerned. Why? For one thing, there is no personal consciousness that may be called yours; consciousness is universal and never private or individual. The hurts and ghosts of the already experienced may well be put to rest and banished from present awareness, yet they, like all else, are held and recorded in the eternal present collective unconscious.

By all means give your shadows a decent burial, enjoy the feeling of release and well-being at a job well done; you walk away a better person. Providing you don't look back, you can enjoy that leaving-the-graveyard feeling. Curiosity of course, having finished with the cat, will in time have its way. One backward glance and you discover your dead and buried shadow walking along right behind, even sometimes having the audacity to lead the way. Being obsessed with the person I think I am is an illness of the mind because seeking my true identity in what I feel as a person, an individual, is asking the mind to truly reflect the mind, which is a bit like looking for myself in a fairground house of mirrors.

Mind is always taking sides, like the drunken man attempting to walk a narrow, straight road. Under the heavy influence of an intoxicating ego, the image reflected is always under the undue influence of present circumstances, feelings, memories, and distorted conclusions. The result of all this hocus pocus is that the "me" that stands up when asked to do so is just one of many waiting in line to claim the privilege of being me; the "me" that emerges victoriously and takes a bow is chosen because its face fits present expectations, desires, fears, and a whole host of other mostly unconscious influences, including memory. Memory colours-in the background, giving the comforting feeling of sameness and familiarity. Memory says, "I have always been this me."

This misleading, yet seductive feeling of always being me is further set in stone by the relative fact that if I am me, then I am not you, or anything else that is not me, which is provided free of charge by an old friend of the me family, duality. The feeling of continuity, which we are convinced comes with being me, is in fact being provided by the witnessing awareness, which is my true identity and eternal nature. It witnesses all, including the frantic activity of the ego that is destined for all its days to seek out, personalise, and take shelter in all experiences so as to ensure its own survival. "Any port in a storm" is what the me always says.

WHEN LISTENING HAPPENS

Once our feet of clay have touched solid, holy ground, we walk back into life in a better way, or maybe it is life that walks back to us. The tail no longer wags the dog, the shadow is no longer taken to be the substance. But this way of being together as one requires a special listening and a different

149

way of being with one another. It requires an uncommon listening that differs greatly from simply hearing, or the kind of listening that we have developed in our everyday conversations. Generally, when we are listening to someone, we may be thinking of something completely different from what the other person is saying. We might also be struggling to have an answer to the other person's problems or we may be impatiently waiting for the other person to finish so that we can have our say. In these cases, we are not listening at all, we are only hearing, or partially listening. To listen properly, there must be no me present, no one who is listening, just listening. This is not as strange or difficult as it might first appear. Remember that peace, quietness, awareness and whole-mindedness are our basic nature, so in listening we don't have to be anything, we can just be. We don't have to be the priest, the doctor, the parent, or the one with the solution. If someone is sharing with me and I am searching for an answer, then I am not listening, or, more correctly, there is no listening. If I think the person should not feel this way or should not be this way, whether they are depressed, paranoid, suicidal or whatever, then there is no true listening taking place. If I wish in any way for the person to be different from the way they are right now, then I am not listening. When I accept that the way they are right now is perfect for right now, then there is listening. When

I see that the way a person or a situation is as the only fact, the only truth right now, then there is nothing to be done, nothing to be changed, except to listen with an open mind and an open heart. In fact, our hearts are always open, they just get obscured by our thinking. When this kind of listening takes place, the person speaking feels no resistance from the listener, they don't have to convince or prove anything because the will of the listener is in abeyance. There is a spiritual space and the speaker is not self-conscious. With no boundary, there is consciousness speaking and consciousness listening. When this happens, a great healing is taking place. Fears, guilt, anger, and old hurts and wounds may emerge from their hiding place in the unconscious, from the divided self, and enter the light and healing of the fully conscious present.

> *Forget every idea of right and wrong any classroom ever taught you*
> HAFIZ

When there is no competition between speaker and listener, not only is a trouble halved but it often melts away in the light of love, leaving only a memory, without the pain to weigh us down. There is a great feeling of lightness and relief which is felt by both parties who have merged together for a moment in love. When the boundaries collapse, there is only love, unconditional, uncreated, unborn and undying. How strange and almost insane a thing it is that to be of real value to one another we are sometimes asked to put aside everything we know, everything we have learnt, all that the information society tells us we must remember. Yet if the brightest person is to be of maximum benefit to the one they love most, to the person who is the love of their life, they have to forget everything they know about everything, and everything they know and think about themselves. Being a child again, they have entered the kingdom of heavenly innocence, their true home, where nothing or no thing is needed, and in this way when everything they take themselves to be is thrown down, it becomes the bridge by which others also can cross to safety.

It is not, of course, that there is anything wrong with knowledge and learning. The accumulation of information and living skills is of immense value in our daily lives, as also is memory and the ability to plan ahead. What is more important, however, is to realise that there is much more to living a life than what takes place in our heads. Our heads are wonderful. But you and I don't live only there. You and I don't live just because our heads exist, we don't only exist because our bodies live. Our bodies exist because you and

I live. It is you as I and I as you together that animate all bodies and all lives in all of life.

Once we start to glimpse our own immensity, our brains and our minds start to take their proper place as useful instruments, and another false god falls by the wayside. Only by coming to realise all that we are not can we shorten the road to what we are. This whole subject of what we really are is, in one way, very simple, yet it is the ultimate challenge. Any challenge we willingly accept to take on (or are thrown into) is to find ourselves on an adventure without really realising where we are going. On all adventure trails, there is some element of danger or surprise. To be adventurous is to be attracted in some way to the unknown. There is little adventure in what we already know and are familiar with. It demands of us to stay open-minded and to face fear, which is to face ourselves. We will, of course, feel much safer if we remain where we are, to stay with what we know. We might at first wonder "why am I doing this?" or "why am I here?", but then, after a while on the trail, all that we were familiar with and were so sure of before takes on a dream-like quality and seems somehow so far away, back there somewhere. Now the real adventure starts. We are also more uncertain than ever of what lies ahead and we now realise that we have come too far to turn back, for to go back is just as uncertain as what may lie ahead. We unwittingly have just discovered true open-mindedness, where we just don't know and, far from being a set-back, we have fallen upon a great treasure, something that is to be of such value for the journey ahead and without which we perhaps could not continue.

To be fair, most of us can say that we are open-minded at one time or another. Of course, there are varying degrees of open-mindedness, and perhaps we have only a very limited choice regarding how open-minded we are. True open-mindedness is no-mindedness and no-mindedness comes about when we arrive at the end of our thinking, and this is something we are gifted with by circumstances rather than by choice. It is a state of no choice, no resistance, no power, in which we are returned to our childlike unpolluted innocence. Can you just imagine the immense difference this state of innocence would make in our daily living—in our relationships with one another and the world about us or the world within us—to walk free of the suffocating drag-net of inherited conditioning, the bitter-sweet gift of ancient societies, which gets handed down by parents to children like an Olympic flame that never quenches? There is a noble beauty and happiness at the core of each and every one of us that we long to touch and hold forever. In our fleeting moments of blissful, self-transcending happiness, we sometimes glimpse that secret life of love and light before the cold hand of earthly life pulls us back to more pressing business. But the earthly hand that rocks us from the cradle is not the only hand that rocks us. As in the old poem, where the dust-covered, unwanted violin was suddenly brought to life by the touch of the master's hand, we too can be awakened from our sleep of earth by a touch of the master's hand, and whether the touch be heavy or light the result is the same in the long run. The heavy-handed crisis in life that brings us to our senses and to the end of our senses is often God's greatest gift without which freedom may not be possible.

PARK BENCH THINKING

The soft brown eyes I found myself looking into that day seemed older than I could imagine, but they might also have been the eyes of a child too young to know he was a child, eyes that reflected no statement of intent but spoke silently of an eternal innocence and something forever free.

Sitting in the warm spring sunshine we were sharing a park bench, when suddenly he began speaking without invitation or preamble as if we had known each other always. "You were deep in thought," he said. "I used to do that, but not anymore. Now I am free from the all capturing darkness of thinking, because now I know that thoughts think themselves into existence, and they also think me into existence. You see, every new thought that comes up brings a new me along with it, so really this me is a ghostly impostor, because if each new thought is also a new me, that means when there is no thought there is no me."

I could see he was in earnest and that the words were coming from somewhere deep within him. "Are you really saying that when there are no thoughts I don't exist," I asked him.

"Well yes and no, you do and you don't, because when a thought comes up there is no thinker of that thought. Remember it is the thought that brings the thinker, and this gives the impression that there is a thinker thinking the thoughts. That's what ego is, and that's also how the feeling of a me doing the thinking gets superimposed upon pure awareness. This awareness is present at all times, before thoughts, during thoughts, and when all thinking has come to an end. This pure awareness is what you love the most but that thief, the ego, keeps stealing your most treasured possession over and over again and is never brought to justice."

"What's this treasured possession you speak of? I like being me, and I want this me to stay alive for as long as possible. What's wrong with that?" He remained perfectly still for a few moments before he answered, as if something was gathering itself together deep within. "There's absolutely nothing wrong with wanting to live, except what you think you want is not really what you want. You see, memory gives the enchanting feeling of continuance, that this me feeling is present at all times and has been for as long as you can remember. It also brings the conviction of you being an individual, and the big problem with that kind of thinking is that the feeling of being me is not present at all times, but comes and goes with each passing thought, and surely you are much more than just a passing thought?"

"I've never entertained this kind of questioning before," I said, "and if what you say is true, then I feel like some kind of fraud because if I am not me then who am I and how can I know who I am without thinking?"

"Now we are getting places. What you really love the most more than anything or anyone else is to be, to be present. This feeling of conscious presence is what has always been with you and you want it to continue always. Well, I have good news for you: it will continue always, and it has been

157

present without interruption eternally. Now, to answer your question about knowing yourself without thinking, remember that self-consciousness, the me, the individual and the thought stream all come into the equation together; one brings the other. Before their arrival you were present and this presence was there prior to all else, and long long before these late arrivals imposed themselves upon pristine awareness, you were at perfect peace, complete in every way without want or need of any kind, because in pure awareness there exists no duality, no subject versus object, and no you versus all that you think is not you, only pure subjectivity. This then is the glory you have always known. Is it any wonder that when you think of yourself as an individual, a separate person, that somehow there seems to be something missing, something lost or forgotten, and you wander through a lifetime accepting gratefully any momentary feelings of happiness, and yet the feelings of something missing always returns. It represents your forgetfulness of your true glory, so now can you see why thinking can't help you because thought can only know all that has been already experienced and never what was prior to all experiences."

I sat, stunned into silence. Again, some rare stillness appeared to take him into itself as he sat like a statue that had been cut from a distant hillside. After some time I heard myself saying "If what you say is true, and strangely I don't feel any resistance to what you have said, yet I still don't understand what it is I need to do?"

"Absolutely nothing," he replied. "If you have understood deep within yourself, within your intuitive intelligence, that what you truly are was never born and so can never die, and that not only is eternal life yours for the taking, but that you are eternal life itself, then what is there to do and who is there to do anything? Speaking absolutely, you have never been any of the things you have taken yourself to be in this earthly world of appearances. You are the conscious presence that witnesses all, including the thought stream. Just remain as the witnessing presence and you will know peace and freedom."

"You mean all I have to do is nothing and just be? That sounds too easy, too simple, there must be a catch."

"In some ways you are right, because what I have told you must be grasped by the intuitive intelligence, which is a far greater intelligence than thought can ever be. When you understand through thought it is never original, and so then it becomes another concept to be collected along with all the others that reinforce the notion that there exists a thinker of the thoughts and a doer who needs to do something. There is nothing to be done, you are already liberated, and already heavenly free."

When he had finished speaking I felt as if everything I had always taken to be important had just walked out on me, and yet I remained unconcerned and at peace. As I opened my eyes I felt all my questioning and needing had gone, and so had the gentle stranger. But he wasn't the only stranger who left that day.

INSIDE OUT IMAGININGS

One morning, half awake and half dressed, I stepped outside to meet the half-brightened new day. Breathing in the cool morning air in an attempt to shake the night out of myself and bring the outside world into focus, it hit me. Suddenly everything was shocked out of itself. The mental framework that had served me so well until now just walked out and left me stranded. Greatly puzzled, I looked around for the familiar, but all that had once comforted me, and all I had once been comfortable with no longer made itself available. That's the trouble with waking up: it arrives unannounced, dispelling unceremoniously all that went before it. It struck me that I had not stepped into an outside world at all. What I had stepped into was an inside world—not an inside as in my body or my head, but into something much less ordinary, and now the boundaries inside and outside the mind and body no longer held any relevance. They had somehow collapsed into themselves and out of themselves. And me? Well, I was no longer me; in fact, there was no me at all because now I had become everything. Not only had I woken from sleep that morning but I had also been awakened from ordinary wakefulness.

> *What miraculous worlds roll within the vast, the all-embracing ocean of the mind*
> RUMI

It's not every day that we wake up twice. Most days we don't wake up at all, but merely change dreams. We dream we are asleep and we dream we are awake. Or perhaps all this dreaming is only a dream anyway, and then every once in a very long while, moving from one dream to another, we miss our step and fall out of our minds. Suddenly our eyes of innocence are restored to us because, after all, we have been here before. Our childlike eyes once held this truth in perfect focus, and that is where I stood that morning. I was neither young nor old, neither inside nor outside the body, not awake nor asleep, neither this nor that. It seemed as if I was nothing in particular because I was everything and everywhere. I was standing in the eternal.

Very strange indeed, this awakening business, or maybe it only appears strange because I had been awoken too suddenly from normal wakefulness. Then what did I do? I walked back out of whatever it was I had just walked into, back into whatever I had walked out of earlier, and then I had a cup of tea.

THE BUTTERFLY

The butterfly landed suddenly out of the early morning sunshine as the caterpillars were busily eating their way through the green leaves. Its unexpected arrival shocked them into stillness and, full of wonder, they asked "What kind of strange creature are you?" "You might find this very strange," replied the butterfly, "but I was once like you, and one day you also will be just as I am. You will no longer have to crawl about in darkness eating bitter leaves but will be able to fly off into the brightness above." The caterpillars accused the butterfly of lying and belittling their way of life, and set upon the brightly coloured creature with such rage that it would never again lift its wings into the warm air of daylight. They then returned to continue with the important business they were accustomed to.

When our one cherished reality is the only one that we are sure off, we expect everyone to march in line. To be out of step is to fall behind and often to be counted out when the marching band of progress marches forward into some future. It is in our own interest to keep up, we are told, or we risk falling into the terrible darkness of failure.

How great a pretender one needs to be to cope with the so-called normality of life is not easy to quantify. Just how low would the butterfly have to stoop before it became accepted by the caterpillars? Was it really asking too much of them to raise their heads and at least try to imagine some other kind of reality that might happily exist along side theirs? Is life for many people, just as for the caterpillars, so straight-lined that only the fittest are able to make it?

WHEN SHADOWS FALL

From the shadows of life, there will sometimes emerge a sadness which, in the words of William Wordsworth, "Doth lie too deep for tears". Not only does it lie too deep for tears but this most private suffering, because of its nature, also lies too deep for thoughts, and therefore too deep for words. This brings us face to face with one of humanity's most frustrating emotional experiences, because it places our every-day means of communication into redundancy. The unfortunate ones who find themselves in this tragic isolation are standing in what can best be described as a nowhere place, a kind of inner desert where all emotional affections fall by the wayside, lost under a whirling storm of negativity. Here in this ghostly landscape, self-identity, self-esteem, and self-worthiness have all walked off into some vaguely remembered distant past. As for the future, it holds no meaning whatsoever because there is only an ever-painful present to be experienced, lending itself relentlessly to the conviction of being a nowhere person. This is a dereliction that is almost impossible to comprehend unless one has personally stood there, and even then for those who are fortunate enough to return, understanding and verbalising what they have been through is greatly hampered by the absence of any adequate frame of reference to which their experiences may be compared. Here, our every-day means of communication fail miserably to reveal what it feels like to be trapped and helpless in a nowhere state of mind.

At this point I feel it important to state that this commentary is not a comprehensive study; its intention is to offer an understanding of one of life's often mortally wounding experiences from a perspective that may not be ordinarily available. For the sufferer who is lost in this unchosen private hell, total powerlessness is their heart-breaking reality, yet despite its intensely private nature, their suffering can also be highly contagious for the family, loved ones, and friends who in their willingness and heartfelt need to help find their best efforts are often neutralised and frustrated out of the equation. Here they come face to face with their own personal powerlessness when attempting to intervene or in some way alleviate the intensely private nature of what ails the person they wish to help. Furthermore, their best attempts to help, or sometimes even to realise that help is needed, are further complicated by the fact that the sufferer in a struggle for survival feels either forced or has become accustomed to acting out a kind of normality role play, which makes helping all the more difficult. This habitual role play masks the sufferer's great inner difficulty in coping with everyday life, something they see others seemingly take in their stride. For the people who innocently find themselves involved in a life that's rapidly losing its colour and worthwhileness, the conviction that the fast-moving train of life is slipping out of reach and may already appear too far gone becomes a reality. For some even, one more day of playing to the gallery of life can become one more day too much. Despite heroic efforts to shore up their wafer-thin version of ordinariness, it slowly disappears under the intense heat of their innermost pain and personal powerlessness. Now being lost in the no-boundary world of their own psyche, feeling imprisoned within their own bodies represents for them being outside help and being helpless. This becomes the jumping-off place for many, where suicide represents for them their only hope of making a break for freedom. No one is responsible for the unfortunate and tragic events that follow, for in the final analysis all are equally powerless. When translated, this means no power, no control, no responsibility, no ifs, buts, maybes, or onlys. This is why personal powerlessness at this level is possibly the darkest, deepest, and most heart-breaking emotional pain we in our humanity are capable of experiencing.

So why is it that we find such difficulty in understanding and accepting powerlessness? Could it be we would rather avoid the subject entirely lest we feel compelled to admit to our own powerlessness, preferring instead to take shelter and comfort in our notions of free will, self-control, will power, and determination. We resent the suggestion our life may not rest as safely and assuredly in our own care as we would like to believe. Furthermore we are convinced that in the more defining moments of life we will have the power to make the right decision, This, of course, is not entirely true, but we think this way because we want to. It furnishes us with the comforting feeling of being in control, and therefore we feel less afraid. We fail to see that these momentous decisions make themselves mostly under the heavy hand of interior and exterior influences preceding and accompanying such events. Were we to take the trouble, we would see that this also holds true in our daily life, where even the more mundane events have, innumerable cause and never stand alone.

Our willingness to live in concepts and beliefs, how we think things are as opposed to how they actually are, is, of course, far more comforting and ego-embellishing than facing the truth; we prefer it that way. But the flow of life has a nasty way of interfering in our most cherished views of how life is, or should be, when it brings to our door events we are seldom adequately prepared for. They arrive uninvited and shockingly announce their presence. When this happens, our much valued and trusted heartfelt emotional values are often scattered to the winds, and we stand in dereliction by the wayside. This is a powerlessness that concedes no ground to our finest thinking or breaking hearts.

We can run, and we may hide, but eventually, if our life is ever again to be worth living, we are compelled to at least become willing and try to accept our painful present reality. For those less fortunate, few such opportunities sadly exist; their plight is often made all the more obscure by the presence of a highly deceptive super-ego, which does not always express itself in the usual mannerisms associated with an exaggerated sense of self-importance; in fact, the very opposite may well be the case, where the super-ego feeds off the drama of misery, self-pity, negativity, and feelings of low self-worth. At the same time, the person may hold the irrational conviction that they have all the answers and know exactly what is best for them, but still remain totally oblivious to their irrationality. Their chances of recovery are further hampered, because awareness of self from an objective view point is denied them by the all-confining scope of their mind-locked existence.

For those fortunate enough to escape, their recovery also

168

greatly depends on the ability to experience a deep and genuine emotional crisis, bringing about ego deflation at a profound level, with the resulting surrender enabling them to ask for help, or at least be open to help. Over these life-changing happenings, the person, of course, remains at all times completely powerless. For all involved, this kind of earth-shattering powerlessness is not easy to accept, and for this no criticism is due. What is within our remit, however, is at least a willingness to accept that some people, even from a young age, are never wholehearted dwellers of the earth. Through no fault of their own they give an emotional value to even the most trivial events of life, coupled with an intense self-consciousness and great emotional sensitivity; their inner private life is seldom a comfortable one. Also accepting our own vulnerability, and not seeing it as some kind of weakness, might result in the presence of a more open heart that hopefully furnishes us with a deeper understanding. Perhaps then, with a new-found humility, we are better able to cope when the darker shadows of life fall our way.

THE POVERTY OF MORE.

Human beings could in some ways be described as "the creatures of the more". If any aspect of our humanity opens a doorway into the shallowness of our egotistic existence, it is our everlasting need for a little bit more .When a child reaches about three and a half--approximately the age when the "me" feeling, the ego, is half-way to fully establishing itself at the centre of all of life's experiences—he or she can often resemble the ultimate obsessive consumer who has lost the run of themselves. Enough is rarely ever enough. Their eyes, we often remind them, are bigger than their stomachs. "I want, I want, I want" is their most frequent refrain, which results in soul pain for the child and trouble in the house. Slowly the parents manage to put what we call manners on the child. This is at best a surface dressing, which acts as veil of acceptability cast upon our inner world of want—"we the creatures of the more"..

Advancing into adulthood, or rather being dragged into adulthood by a quickly growing body, the wanting child learns the art of deception, making a spit-and-polish attempt at giving a respectable face to his or her more hidden aspects, but the inner child is not vanquished by the onset of terminal adulthood. Because, from the other side of the veil, a little voice cries out for more: more love, more security, more affection, more time before I die, more life after death. Oh, and please remember me when I am gone.

The problem with "we creatures of the more" is that enough is never enough for very long. Why? Because it's not the thing I want that's causing the problem, it's the wanting itself. When I want, I hurt. It's no good using my head to solve the problem, because heads are for important, grown-up kind of people. No, for this work,

> *Peace can not be reached by the simple addition of pluses and elimination of minuses from life*
> WILLIAM JAMES

only hearts will do. Remember that before the age of three and a half, all childhood businesses is heart business only. The poverty of wanting comes with thought, which is head business. Before this, there is no wanting once the basic needs have been met. Then slowly the ego, the "me" feeling, gets established, and that's when heart-living gets gradually left behind and almost forgotten in favour of head-living. Here, the ever needy ego takes the ever-wanting child as its foster child. This is head life, not that there is anything wrong with living from our heads, providing we don't move in, lock the door, and draw the blinds. When this happens, heart-living gets left behind in life's shadows and gradually becomes almost forgotten and, for a while, not even missed.

The savage, it is said, loves his native shore; we the creatures of the more who have become exiles unwittingly are no different, longing unconsciously to set foot on our native shore, where our hearts once again become the centre of our being. Here, head-life and heart-life are not poles apart, where one is lost and the other forgotten, because here in the heart of total living all aspects of life are complementary; here heart and head live together in friendship; one is the window to humanity, and the other is what makes humanity possible.

Together, heart and head represent wholeness, completeness. The heart speaks intuitively, while the head speaks intellectually. Intuitive awareness represents total intelligence emerging from the heart of life itself; intellectual intelligence, on the other hand, emerges out of thought, which is just one aspect of total intelligence. The truth is we never get lost in life itself; rather we get lost amongst the myriad contents of life. We become dazzled, amused, and amazed by the power of thinking and by all that appears to lie outside of thought--what we call the objective or the real world, which is real only so long as we are able to think it real. A day may dawn, however, when, finding ourselves away off shore, we realise that thought is not the most seaworthy vessel to risk our lives in. When our heads let us down we are forced to seek shelter. If the winds of change blow in our favour, there is always the chance of returning home to ourselves, a place of rest for the restless and one-time creatures of the more.

WORDS, SPIRITUALITY, AND TRUTH

Words are not facts and still less are they the primordial fact. If we take them too seriously we shall lose our way in a forest of entangling briars. We need to be startled out of our habitual complacency from the home-made verbal universe in which we do most of our living—Aldous Huxley.

Living as we mostly do in a world created by words, we blissfully spend our time like children building castles on the seashore, every grain of sand gladly lending itself to the creation of a reality that only the child can know. But in making our way through a verbal universe, we often find ourselves, as Aldous Huxley says, lost in a forest of briars, becoming entangled in a reality of our heads' making and divorced from our absolute truth. In this bewitching exile, which is at best a relative reality, our words make concepts and concepts present themselves as truth. When housed in a conceptual way, vulnerability and restlessness become our constant companions, seldom allowing us to draw an easy breath. Escaping now and then from our heads, we take comfort wherever we can find it and feel relieved. All, however, is not well, for lurking in the shadows of our conceptualising, vulnerability, and restlessness lies fear, which we are constantly in flight from. Thus in times of total powerlessness our choices are few, and for some this is where the road tragically runs out. When life itself, for whatever reason, loses its value and charm, the universe seems to no longer act in our favour but becomes hostile and threatening, leaving us with the feeling of being left behind as the ever-moving train of life speeds off.

The hard truth about this, however, is that what has failed us is not life itself but our idea of life. It is our concepts and word-constructed philosophies that fail to shelter us when the storm-force winds rip through the landscape of our lives. Words are fair-weather friends who are never around when we need them the most. Words are not things; at best they describe, or distort, what already is. The reality that words suggest is only relative to the words that are used and can never stand independently as truth. When words become the ground on which we build our earthly home, we unknowingly find ourselves on very shaky foundations.

To rely on words and thoughts only is to forget the heart—the centre of our being—and to relegate our feelings, emotions, and sense of ourselves, the building blocks of our spirituality, to second place. Thoughts, of course, think themselves independently into existence, and it is not we who think thoughts. If you are convinced that the opposite is true, sit down quietly to stop all thinking and see how far you get. If I am the creator of the thoughts, it must naturally follow that I should always be able to think thoughts that will guarantee my happiness at all times, which, of course, is impossible, even if I am blessed with a positive attitude.

What then is a person supposed to do when thinking walks out on them, taking all they feel they are as a person right along with it? After all, it is with the sense of self that I bring the colour to my life and without which my life would be cold and meaningless. If this is now my sorry state, my alienation is further compounded by the fact that my ability to communicate my feelings is also gone. When all I have taken myself to be is housed and sheltered in thought I am like a person in some endless ocean whose survival depends on a piece of driftwood.

Living my life on the surface of consciousness is living on the level of the ego only, where my reality is based solely on thought. In such a situation I run the risk of becoming lost, unable to reach out for help and where others cannot reach in to help me. This sad state is, in itself, a death, for wherever I look all others are participating in some kind of distant reality that I am divorced from and feel unable to touch. Alienation and powerlessness are now my constant companions, and out of conditioning and memory I may still act out some two-bit part in the theatre of life, which allows me to survive in some shallow, meaningless way. But in a fast-moving world a shallow life soon gets pushed into hopelessness.

When someone loses their way in life no one is to blame, neither the one who is lost, nor those who remain behind. If something could have been done, it would have done itself, for this is the nature of life; life loves to live, and love cannot help but love. Sometimes our overburdening sense of responsibility can blind us to the truth and in turn increases the weight of the personal cross we drag after us through life. This obscures even more our sense of what or who we really are. When our life as we know it is defined by the content of all our experiences alone, we visit a great injustice upon ourselves. We become slaves to the ego, which de-

176

pends on past experiences for its very existence and is always placing itself at the centre of all of life's events, thus ensuring its own survival.

This, of course, is all taking place at the level of thought and memory—which is also thought—and now we have arrived back to the very point we started from: that is, how off-balance a life can be when we expect our heads to supply us with everything necessary to live an earthly life. What happens is that we become serial abusers of the gifts our god-like nature supplies us with, and in the same way that addicts abuse the substance they have become dependent on, we abuse the blessings of thought, becoming addicted to the point where thought becomes our master, blinding us to the immensity of our true spiritual nature. The tail now wags the dog, and we become subservient to the ego and thinking, which is a good servant but a bad master.

When for some reason, or even for no apparent reason, we get into trouble psychologically, and if we have always depended on our thinking for guidance, we can find ourselves in big trouble, where fear, anxiety, bewilderment, and hopelessness surround us completely. For some, escape may come in the shape of an emotional crisis which brings about complete ego deflation, and in this brief window of opportunity we are once again open to help from those around us. The sad news, however, is that the road to the hell of our psyche has not many roundabouts and only the lucky few are able for the road back to a better, more balanced way of life where thinking and the ego become part of our story and not the whole of it. Life may then be lived from the centre of our being, our true spiritual nature.

How different life would be if we could only allow ourselves to reach out for that part of our being that never will forsake us nor let us down in our darkest hours. To be touched by it, or to allow it to touch us, a little humility is necessary. This can be induced by surrendering our own importance, starting the day by saying "Today I surrender my will and my life and I will try to accept whatever comes my way at any given moment." This may sound like I am no longer in control of my own life, and that is exactly what is required because it is the fight to stay in control that is killing me. It is as if I am in quicksand: the more I struggle the further I sink. If, however, I remain still and ask for help the chances are it will come my way. This is responding, rather than reacting, to pain. When I respond to pain it means I am trying to accept it, to acknowledge that it exists, so I don't make it worse and add further mental anguish. The possibility of my recovery is greatly enhanced by responding. On the other hand, when I react I am turning my back on the pain and attempting to escape, which unconsciously makes the pain worse because I am now in conflict. A reaction always create further reactions, which equals more pain, thus bringing about a situation of conflict that is far more difficult to cope with than the original problem.

Here we do well to remember that powerlessness means having no power and that hopelessness means having no hope. Yet we still think that if only those for whom life no longer holds any relevance could say something or just ask for help, then things would be different.

What we are failing to grasp is that to do this requires some kind of awareness of what is happening inside my head. But how does someone who is lost in their psyche, lost in thought, become aware? If awareness was there they would not be lost in the first place. Remember our sense of individuality is a feeling brought to us courtesy of thought, and thought is exactly what is now the trouble. So expecting someone in great inner pain to talk about their situation is nonsense. It is obvious we are expecting too much and we are trying to understand what is happening from our standpoint only. Unless we have stood in some nowhere place where anything we might cling to for safety has drifted out of reach, then surely we cannot expect to truly understand.

During the period when I found myself lost in an inward nowhereness, even answering the simplest question was painful because thinking and thoughts seemed so far off and did not make themselves easily available for communication. Also at that time I was not aware of the condition I was in. I was just in it. I felt all the feelings associated with my plight but had no insight into these nor any idea of how I might change what was happening. The sense of isolation and negativity was great and was then followed by such an all-enveloping fear that I was unable to leave my bedroom for some time. Then one evening I awoke to find my sister, who lived in England, standing by my bedside. At first I thought I had to be dreaming but then she hugged and kissed me, and for the first time in years I broke down and cried uncontrollably. Within a few hours the doctor was at my bedside and I was in a state of being where others could help me. The next morning I was admitted to a psychiatric hospital and although I felt it was the end of my life I was willing to do whatever was suggested.

And yes, it was the end of my old life—but it was also the beginning of a new one. I had experienced total ego deflation and found myself in an almost childlike state in so far as I felt I was in a state of innocence, without any defensiveness or feelings of self-importance. Pain had driven me to the border and I had somehow found myself on the other side and was free—not that there were to be no more challenges or painful situations, but somehow I was more able to cope with them, and this time on life's terms rather than on mine alone. A comforting feeling of being at ease came about me. I felt safe and no longer isolated from those who loved me. Little did I know then of the adventures that lay ahead. I was already on a spiritual journey to myself, or to that part of self that represented the very heart of my being, and the very heart of our collective existence and non-existence.

Be kind to your sleeping heart. Take it out into the vast fields of light and let it breathe

HAFIZ

Somebody once said that if they ever got to Heaven it would be because they were running from Hell. Perhaps this may be the case for most of us on our earthly journey. The many and various troubles that life brings to our door can at once be a blessing and a curse, depending, one could say, on the fall of the dice, for no event can take place in our living world of relativity without the cooperation of thousands of other events. Not even the most insignificant event or experience can stand alone despite the autonomous way in which it presents itself to our consciousness. Life lives us into existence and out of existence. The notion that it is I who live what I call my life is bewitching indeed, but intense investigation will show it to be untrue. Maybe the reason why tragic events of life often break our hearts is that we are convinced that we are in control, a feeling that brings along with it what we call responsibility, whether for past or future events. These notions and convictions, of responsibility and so-called free will, become the nails that hold together the heavy cross borne by humanity. They are misplaced, serving only to evict us from our proper place in the greater, universal flow of life.

Many of us often carry a heavy burden that really is not ours to carry. It is like in the old story of the traveller who got a lift in a passing donkey and cart and then noticed that the driver had a heavy bag on his back. When the traveller asked him why he did this, the man replied that he didn't like to put all the weight on the donkey. It is a notion that still prevails, that it is we who should take the full burden of life's difficult events and experiences, struggling on alone, and seldom if ever giving due respect to the universal mind of consciousness. So imbedded can this become that it often drives us out of our minds, and tragically for some there is no returning. For most people it becomes a hit and miss affair, yet others breeze through life without even a backward glance. For those who find themselves on the high road to the wastelands of inner turmoil, a grey darkness falling in all directions appears to obscure any possible return to safety.

All, however, is not lost, for there is still one friend who has not abandoned you: the light that shone through your eyes in childhood innocence. Your attention has been captured by thought, but still you are safe because nothing you have taken to be yourself is what you are. The body you say is yours belongs to the universe. It is not sinful and it is not lower than the highest. It has neither father nor mother. Take good care of it because it is an orphan and a gift from Mother Earth. Everything you are aware of is not you, everything that happens in your head is not who you are and is not what you are. If you feel lost and isolated it is because you have taken thoughts to be your personal thoughts. They are not; they think themselves into existence out of consciousness. This is the nature of consciousness; it is not your nature. This consciousness is not your private property, for it is available to all. Neither is your heart the property of the head but is sometimes taken prisoner by thought. Once you hear this you are free, but in truth you are always free. You have forgotten momentarily your birthright and your true self. You have compared your inside feelings with those of others outside and have felt inferior. Or perhaps you have felt superior to others and in doing so have become trapped in an ego that is never satisfied. Again, that is not who you are, nor what you are. But do not be afraid, because your heart will keep you safe always.

What, then, are you to do? The answer is nothing, because trying to do something only intensifies the isolation and strengthens the already rampant ego. Nothing bad will happen; you are perfect just the way you are. Remember there is no such thing as normal. The idea of a collective normality is a crime against nature. What does exist is abounding uniqueness, where differences are the universal rule and not the exception. Your very uniqueness is your blessing from the universe, so honour it by acceptance, and thus compassion. In so doing you are living from your heart, your true home. All the help you may need will come your way. You do not have to strive for it. When you begin to draw an easy breath, all will come to you. You are perfect right now and you are not lost, it only feels like you are. You are not wrong because there is neither wrong nor right, it's just the way it is.

Looking out on the world and comparing yourself to others is a sickness in itself. Leave yourself and others alone, turning away from the inner critic by declaring "What is happening in my head is not my business." In that moment you are free and living from your heart, your spiritual home. Neither is it necessary for you to believe in anything. Just give your true self a break and it will stand shoulder to shoulder with you. Don't judge yourself. Your true nature will never judge you, because spirit cannot judge but only love. Love is its very nature, and this is what you are. Know that you are free and perfect, so draw an easy breath, for you live in the very midst of a loving heart.

In the end, it seems, there is no real observer behind it all — it is the dream of an ultimate observer — a place of final refuge — that blocks the light. When observing stops, the Real appears — crystal clean and empty.

Made in the USA
Charleston, SC
11 January 2016